don't think pink

what *really* makes women buy—
and how to increase your share
of this crucial market

L I S A   J O H N S O N

A N D R E A   L E A R N E D

AMACOM AMERICAN MANAGEMENT ASSOCIATION
NEW YORK □ ATLANTA □ BRUSSELS □ CHICAGO □ MEXICO CITY
SAN FRANCISCO □ SHANGHAI □ TOKYO □ TORONTO □ WASHINGTON, D.C.

Special discounts on bulk quantities of AMACOM books are available to corporations, professional associations, and other organizations. For details, contact Special Sales Department, AMACOM, a division of American Management Association, 1601 Broadway, New York, NY 10019.
Tel.: 212-903-8316. Fax: 212-903-8083. Web site: www.amacombooks.org

This publication is designed to provide accurate and authoritative information in regard to the subject matter covered. It is sold with the understanding that the publisher is not engaged in rendering legal, accounting, or other professional service. If legal advice or other expert assistance is required, the services of a competent professional person should be sought.

Library of Congress Cataloging-in-Publication Data

Johnson, Lisa, 1967-
  Don't think pink : what really makes women buy—and how to increase your share of this crucial market / Lisa Johnson, Andrea Learned.
    p. cm.
Includes bibliographical references and index.
  ISBN 0-8144-0815-X
  1. Women consumers. 2. Marketing. I. Learned, Andrea. II. Title.

HC79.C6J64 2004
658.8'34'082—dc22

2004005393

Printing number
10 9 8 7 6 5 4 3

TO OUR PARENTS—
LARRY AND JOYCE,
DAVID AND MURIEL

ACKNOWLEDGMENTS

As first-time authors, we began to think about how many people we wanted to thank and our heads almost exploded. Just as those celebrities that take the stage at awards ceremonies, we want to say, in advance, that anyone who has helped us along this path that we forgot to list below—please blame it on our aging brains and not on our lack of appreciation! Onward—

We dedicated the book to our parents, in recognition of all their amazing support. The next in line to thank would certainly be Lisa's wonderful husband, Dave, and our siblings: Kris, Julia, Claudia and Bill.

Then, there are the editors and amazing staff at AMACOM, including Ellen Kadin, Andrew Ambraziejus, Dianne Estridge—and the outstanding copy editor with whom we had the privilege to work, Charles Levine. You brought so much to this process, including amazing talent, much experience, lots o' humor, math skills(!!), attention to detail and dedication. You didn't just make *Don't Think Pink* good—you made writing it fun!

Friends and colleagues whose support went beyond compare: Carey Kerns, Glen Berry, Nicole Williams, Ann Handley, Jami York, Jackie Huba and Joy Stauber.

In no particular order—those people who may or may not have had anything to do with the book, but whose influence and support have prepared us for such a task:

Lindsey Pollak, Helen Thompson, Robin Ireland, Romney Gibson, Tutti McCormick, Robyn Knox, Rachel Johnson, Brook Jones, Dani Jansen, Lindsey Black, Amy Smith, Candace Carson, Annie Leonard Shannahan, Alexis Gutzman, Carole McClendon, Steve Sarner, Daniel Fogg, Shaun Davidson, Ray Palys, Galie Jean-Louis, Mike Consol, Marti Barletta, Jodi Turek, Aliza Sherman, Eileen Brady (for tipping us off on "tipping"), Melody Biringer, Linda Gosch, Cheri Hansen.

And finally, we'd like to acknowledge one another and our shared faith in God. It takes so much more than a village to write a book.

contents

FOREWORD VII

PREFACE IX

1 BRAIN TRAINING
How Not to Think Pink 1

2 NOW YOU SEE "HER"
The Visible Approach to Marketing to Women 25

3 NOW YOU DON'T (SEE "HER")
The Transparent Approach to Marketing to Women . . . 34

4 INSIDE A WOMAN'S MIND
The Scientific Underpinnings 62

5 SHAPING THE GENERATIONS
Baby Boomers (and Matures) to Gen Yers 83

6 LOOKING BEYOND GENERATIONS
The Buying Filters of Life Stages and Roles 114

7 CULTURAL INFLUENCERS

The Buying Filters of Emerging Majorities. 139

8 LEARNING CURVES AND LIFE STAGES

Relationship-Building Opportunities 155

9 THE INTERNET-SAVVY WOMAN

Connecting with Her Online. 172

10 ONLINE RESEARCH

Using E-Marketing to See Women Clearly 187

**11 ENLISTING WOMEN AS YOUR
MARKETING PARTNERS**

An Alliance for Brand Success 198

**AFTERWORD: INVESTING IN A
TRANSPARENT FUTURE** 211

NOTES 215

RECOMMENDED READING. 223

INDEX 225

foreword

More than a decade ago—a long time before I worked with marketers—I participated in a focus group for a new brand of dog food aimed at senior canines.

The manufacturer was particularly interested in what women like me thought of the packaging: Did we find it appealing? Would it inspire a second look on the grocery store shelf? The pet food company sought our input, the focus group leaders explained, since it had identified women as the major purchasers of dog provisions.

Good for them for recognizing women as the target customers. In that, they were way ahead of the curve. But guess what? They fell into some tired old assumptions about packaging, and the bag was an off-putting pastel pink.

"Do women relate to the softer packaging colors?" the group leaders queried.

"Uh, no," we replied.

In *Don't Think Pink*, authors Lisa Johnson and Andrea Learned call this sort of obvious stereotype "pink thinking." Like that dog food company, marketers are often working from antiquated assumptions. They frequently slap pastels and flowers on packaging, or produce "lighter" versions of original products, in a quick-fix effort to appeal to one of today's fastest-growing consumer segments: women.

It's true. Women spend over two trillion consumer dollars a year.

Yet only a fraction of that market can name a brand that speaks to their needs.

Can you sense the opportunity?

Since you are reading this book, I'm guessing that you get what the authors mean when they say that shortsighted marketing causes companies to miss huge opportunities. Just as women's societal roles, and their effect on the economy, have greatly shifted, so too must marketing's approach to serving them.

It's not about appealing to the sensibilities of women—those efforts only scratch the surface. It's more about designing a subtler and more sophisticated approach—Lisa and Andrea call this "transparent marketing"—that can truly inspire women to become loyal customers.

Is this a huge challenge? You bet it is.

But here's the good news: You've already begun. You're reading this book.

Within these pages, the authors have produced both a road map and a resource to help brands reach far beyond "pink thinking." With its accessible how-to format and to-the-point writing, this book tells you how to build cases and campaigns to better meet the needs of your women customers.

In doing so, Lisa and Andrea have not merely produced a credible text, they've also established themselves as pioneers of sorts in marketing to women. I especially love the snappy writing—be sure to read their hilarious recipe in chapter one for "Pink Thinking Formula: "One part limited staff power and budget, two parts internal resistance to new ideas . . . ."

Talk about a marketing Molotov cocktail.

So congratulations on accepting the challenge. Best of luck, and remember, "Think Pink."

Not!

Ann Handley, Editor in Chief, MarketingProfs.com

preface

The fact that women make or influence the majority (roughly 80 percent) of consumer purchases today is old news by now. But how do you leverage this information? What portion of the women's market truly is your market? How can you develop strategies that are authentic for women and relevant in their lives?

This book will show you how to see through the eyes of women—wherever they are in their buying process. Part of this marketing mind training involves learning how women's minds work and what may be influencing their buying behavior. Then comes the really hard part: meeting your women customers on their own terms and forging lasting relationships with them over time.

As marketers, we are schooled in how to read the data and when to hold focus groups. We can quote "the customer is always right," while at the same time trying to develop a marketing strategy from inside the product out. But, becoming a part of the conversations of women as they go about their daily routines is only possible if we return to the roots of good overall marketing and examine our task from a customer-centric perspective—from inside the customer out.

Over time, it's possible to lose touch with who really buys your product, why they buy it over other brands, what is going on in their lives when they choose to make the purchase, and how they feel about their interactions with your customer service staff. Reading this book will help ground you in the strategy development process by getting back to the basics. If your data says your customers are mainly educated women between the ages of 25 and 45, that just isn't enough information on which to proceed. You need to dig in deeper and examine how those women live, what roles they play, what life stages drive them, what cultural experiences influence them, and much more.

Though the book's topic is gender specific, much (if not all) of what we propose herein will serve as a useful reminder and re-training manual for marketing to any of the customer bases in your industry. Understanding the types or profiles of your customers (in this case, women) is key—as is paying attention to their technology confidence levels, and, ultimately, learning to reach them transparently.

Your brand and your marketing team must be authentically interested in, and connected with, the women you serve in order to develop the most resonant products, services and marketing campaigns. The idea is to know your prospective and current women customers so well that you can place your brand right where it needs to be and ensure that your products or services will be readily accessible, in their minds and on the shelf, just when and where they need them.

Reaching women consumers is not a trend. It's the lucrative future, for anyone who grabs it. Slightly tweaked male-oriented products or marketing efforts will no longer do. Once you've read this book and examined your brand by peering through a woman's lens, the need for different ways to reach them as consumers will become clear—and as you re-examine and re-connect with the women who are your current customers, the changes you will need to make should emerge fairly quickly.

Re-entering into conversations with your best and most influential customers is the best way to create products and services that resonate, and the best way to expand on their trust in your brand. Learning to see from a woman's perspective is the key.

CHAPTER 1

brain training

how not to think pink

WOMEN'S SPENDING power and influence were once neglected by companies doing business in the United States. But no longer. The big news over the past few years has businesses scrambling after the now well-documented larger wallets of women transforming the marketplace. With trillions of dollars the prize, companies are looking to overcome the biggest obstacle to their success, something we define as "thinking pink"—an often limited and stereotype-driven view of one of the biggest marketing opportunities in history.

What Is Thinking Pink?

The best way to understand thinking pink may be to revisit the quirky 1999 film *Blast From the Past,* a comedy about people emerging from a thirty-five-year time warp. The movie opens in 1962 at a cocktail party in the home of Calvin and Helen Webber (Christopher Walken and Sissy Spacek), where some of the guests are whispering about how brilliant, but weird, Calvin is. Suddenly President John F. Kennedy appears on TV to announce there are Soviet missiles in Cuba aimed at U.S. targets. Calvin hustles the guests out the door and hurries his pregnant wife into an elevator down to his amazing bomb shelter, where fish grow in breeding tanks and the decor of their aboveground home has been reproduced right down to the lawn furniture.

A brain from Cal Tech, Calvin has been waiting for years for the big one to drop. His prudence is admirable but his luck bad: There's no nuclear war, but a plane crashes into his house, sending a fireball down the elevator shaft, convincing him the war is on. So he closes the steel doors and informs Helen that the time locks won't open for thirty-five years "to keep us from trying to leave." In the sealed atmosphere of the bomb shelter far below Los Angeles nothing changes. Calvin and Helen watch kinescopes of old Jackie Gleason programs, with tuna casseroles on the menu. They raise their son Adam in the ideals of their generation.

While the family lives in their time capsule belowground, out in the daylight Los Angeles develops into a radically different society. When their thirty-five-year-old son Adam ventures aboveground for the first time to replenish supplies and scout the war-torn land, he demonstrates a serious case of early 1960s thinking, completely off for the 1990s.

Today, women's roles in society and their effects on the economy have greatly shifted, catching by surprise companies also stuck in a time capsule, doing business as usual. Women have changed. And, the rules have changed too.

When companies work from tired data, assumptions or stereotypes of what women want (thinking pastels, flowers or "lighter" versions of the original), the results are pink products, marketing campaigns and service offerings that don't connect with today's savvy and empowered women. Pink efforts just scratch the surface of women's desires and often miss the mark altogether.

Business journalist Hillary Chura in *Advertising Age* calls for a more sophisticated approach to women consumers: "Like nervous teenage boys at a junior high dance, marketers haven't figured out how to talk to women, who comprise 51 percent of the U.S. population."[1] With women spending over two trillion dollars each year, enormous growth potential and millions of dollars await companies that do take the time to get it right.

Pink thinking is not a single attitude or action; instead, it is a recipe for weak profits and missed opportunities:

Pink Thinking Recipe

□ One part dated assumptions and information

□ Two parts superseded stereotypes

□ One part limited staff and budget

□ Two parts internal resistance to new ideas

□ Three parts fear of turning off men and making expensive mistakes

□ A generous dollop of pastels, butterflies, hearts and flowers

□ And a double shake of good intentions and sincerity

Do not stir or integrate with other departments. Serve to women customers.

As you can imagine, pink campaigns feel like a patronizing pat on the head for many women. But, don't misunderstand our point: It is not that companies are deliberately setting out to think pink, to underestimate women, or patronize or alienate them. Our own experiences as marketing consultants demonstrate that many, many companies have awakened to the opportunity, yet remain in need of strategies to respond effectively in order to increase their market share among women.

Don't Think Pink was written because the marketplace has changed and we recognize that companies are sincerely looking to better meet the needs of their women customers. This book is designed as a resource and a roadmap to help brands go beyond thinking pink.

---

several cousins of pink thinking

Where any given market has dramatically shifted, as things have in the women's market, the equivalent of pink thinking can happen. We can recognize similar challenges and opportunities in these other lucrative market segments:

SENIOR DISCOUNT THINKING

Marketing to the maturing generation means addressing the growing unpopularity of senior discount thinking. As the "forever young" Baby Boomers reach their retirement years, they are reinventing aging and rejecting traditional symbols of growing older. Companies that have created senior programs will need to completely rethink their approach if they hope to capture the loyalty, affection and business of this new breed of grandparents. Kohler, the maker of kitchen and bath fixtures, for example, gets it. They introduced gorgeous new products that take into consideration an aging person's needs—such as higher toilets and more accessible bathtubs—marketing them simply as the latest innovations. There's not even a hint of senior thinking in the hip new products. The result? Aging Boomers have made these new product lines bestsellers.

GRADE SCHOOL THINKING

Marketing has had to make wholesale changes to keep up with the sophistication of global tweens (eight- to fourteen-year-olds). It has been easy to underestimate the savvy and highly developed preferences of today's sophisticated tween consumers. For years marketers would draw on their own experiences as children and use outdated research and learning methods to determine the best new products and marketing programs for tweens. This grade school thinking forgets that tweens are one of the most sophisticated groups of consumers in the marketplace, and that kids this age have zero tolerance for being treated like children. They just won't be underestimated. While technology companies have honed in on this trendsetting group and pioneered innovations to reach them, the fashion industry is playing catch-up as tweens demand adult fashions in smaller sizes. Slow-changing manufacturers are just waking up to the sophisticated tastes of today's tweens.

CHURCHY THINKING

Segments of the Christian publishing and gift industry seem to be stuck in a time warp, catering to people's desires for spiritual growth by utilizing marketing approaches and preferences of an aging generation. You might say some segments of this industry suffer from churchy thinking. Gone are the days when a store can be filled with "manna mints" and flowery-covered devotion books alone. Contemporary Christian music is an example of a successful segment of that marketplace that has undergone an aggressive makeover and is striking a resonant chord with believers across the nation. Bands like Jars of Clay, Third Day and DC Talk are marketed with the same relevance and savvy of other popular music bands on the billboard charts.

"JUNE CLEAVER" THINKING

"June Cleaver" thinking makes today's moms feel like failures and sets up an ideal that women can no longer meet. June Cleaver was the stereotypical mother and housewife in the 1950s sitcom hit *Leave It to Beaver*. The initial response to June Cleaver thinking was that working women tried to become supermoms, cherishing memories of motherhood in the 1950s, no matter how their own moms did it. All the while these same women were pioneering new opportunities in the workplace. But a twenty-first-century mom's life bears no resemblance to June Cleaver's. Thus, women resent what they know is unattainable and have abandoned June Cleaver aspirations, conducting their lives the way their current environment permits. Advertising campaigns like Dodge Caravan's "What idiot came up with 'stay-at-home moms'?" and AT&T's "Working mom stays connected at the beach" are hitting the right note with today's moms.

HOW TO MOVE BEYOND THINKING PINK

Pink thinking begins inside an organization and expresses itself in the marketplace through products, advertising and marketing programs aimed at women. The following ten steps detail an inside-out approach to helping companies move beyond pink thinking and into a position of brand leadership. When a company can create a brand that reflects a deep knowledge, commitment and understanding of the community of women they serve, women will reward the authenticity of their efforts at the checkout counter.

1. Understand Her Earning Power

Women now earn one trillion dollars a year and their incomes over the past three decades have increased a dramatic 63 percent after inflation, while men's median income has barely budged (+0.6 percent after inflation).[2] This increase in earning power is not the result of one big event but has been fueled by a series of important changes in the workplace, family and personal lives of women. Here are some of the key factors that may contribute to her thicker wallet:

WAGE GAP SHRINKING

The wage gap is quickly narrowing to make women's incomes more comparable to those of their male counterparts, with the average full-time working woman now earning 76 cents on each dollar earned by a man. This is particularly so for the younger generation, where there is the least discrepancy between the wages of men and women, to the tune of just a few cents on the dollar. In 1998, women ages 25–34 earned 83 cents on the male dollar; women ages 19–24, 89 cents on the male dollar.[3]

ADVANCED DEGREES

It's no surprise that college degrees are helping propel women into higher paying professions and executive-level positions. The advancement in women's earning power is powerfully illuminated by their taking home the majority of bachelor degrees (57 percent) and pursuing advanced degrees in record numbers—earning 50 percent of law degrees, 40 percent of MBAs and 46 percent of medical degrees.[4]

HOUSEHOLD INCOME

Women now bring in half or more of the household income in the majority of U.S. households. In the 55 percent of U.S. households made up of married couples, Census Bureau survey data indicates that 48 percent of the working wives provide at least half of household income.[5] But don't forget the influence of the many unmarried women in the United States today. In fact, 27 percent of U.S. households are headed by a single female who brings in the entire household income.[6] One final surprising statistic about women's influence on household income: Among married female executives with a rank of VP or higher in a Fortune 500 company, 75 percent out-earned their husbands, bringing home on average 68 percent of household income.[7]

BUSINESS OWNERSHIP

To achieve this noticeable increase in their contribution to household income, more and more women use their college and advanced degrees to start or buy their own businesses. In fact, women own 40 percent of all companies in this country. From 1987 to 1999, the number of women-owned businesses grew 103 percent, about one and a half times the national average. What's more, their employment levels grew 320 percent and the revenues of these women-owned companies grew most of all, up 436 percent. Of course, these strides translate into bigger paychecks and higher overall net worth.

HIGH NET WORTH

Women head approximately 40 percent of the households with assets of more than $600,000 and have quietly become the majority asset holders in the United States, controlling 51 percent of the private wealth in this country.[8] In addition, Mature and Baby Boomer women (who statistically will live longer than their male siblings and spouses) will benefit the most from the intergenerational transfer of wealth from their parents. The ranks of affluent women will only increase, and it is estimated by 2010 that two-thirds of all private wealth in the United States will rest in their hands.

2. Wake Up to Her Spending Power

Perhaps even more compelling than women's increased earning power is their spending power in their households and workplaces. While women's combined earnings are estimated around $1 trillion

annually, her spending power overall is estimated at over $2 tril-
lion each year.[9]

HOUSEHOLD PURCHASING AGENT

No one could deny, once they've given it any thought at all, that
women are responsible for the bulk of consumer purchases. The
proof is in the numbers: Women account for roughly 80 percent
of all consumer buying. The Center for Women's Business
Research indicates that businesswomen (working women and
female entrepreneurs) are the primary decision makers in households, making 95 percent of the purchasing decisions. To be more
specific and drive home that point: Women are responsible for 70
percent of all travel decisions, 57 percent of all consumer electronics purchases, and they buy 50 percent of all new vehicles (influencing 80 percent of overall automobile sales).[10] Finally, women
write an estimated eight out of ten personal checks in the United
States, making their financial power even more formidable.[11]
Women in most households today not only control the spending
of their own paychecks, but a good deal of their husband's as well.

CORPORATE PURCHASING AGENT

The number of women in business or who own their own business
means that the buying power of women extends beyond household
spending to corporate spending as well. Business product vendors
are noticing that 51 percent of all purchasing managers and agents
are women.[12] Furthermore, human resources executives are pre-
dominately women, and they make the key decisions for corporate
financial services, including lucrative insurance contracts and company retirement plans.

Office managers are the important filters for a company's supplies
and services as well. The recent UPS ad campaign "What can Brown
do for you?" tapped into the reality that women office managers are
the key decision makers who choose and use their services.

how women got to be so important to the U.S. economy: societal changes and economic realities

WOMEN TAKE CARE OF BUSINESS

During World War II, many women entered the workforce for the first time to assist the war effort. Because so many of them discovered they enjoyed working outside the home, a fundamental shift in women's attitudes toward conventional life paths ensued. Then, during the 1960s and 1970s women started to enter the workforce in large numbers, in part because of the newfound sense of freedom they had gained though the various activist movements. The introduction of the birth control pill also had a significant effect on women's role in business, as it gave them a choice of when, and if, they wanted to have children.

WOMEN OWN BUSINESSES

Between 1997 and 2002, sales generated by women-owned firms increased 40 percent nationwide, nearing $1.5 trillion. And, according to the U.S. Census Bureau, women-owned firms employed nearly 9.2 million workers as of 2002. Furthermore, this wealthy growth segment of businesspeople also influences the purchasing of many business-related products and professional services. The U.S. Small Business Administration reports that women-owned businesses generate more than the gross domestic product of most countries, contributing $2.38 trillion annually in revenues to the U.S. economy! And this trend is no fluke. *Working Mother* magazine predicts these numbers will continue to grow as women-owned businesses open at twice the rate of male-owned enterprises.[13]

WOMEN INVEST

With an increasing number of women investing in the stock market, the women's demographic will create more wealth in the future. According to the National Association of Securities Dealers, women now comprise 47 percent of investors overall, 50 percent of new and potential shareholders and 35 percent of investors with holdings of more than $50,000 in mutual funds and stocks. We call this nest egg building, and then some!

SINGLE WOMEN CREATE NEW BUYING DYNAMICS

Seventy percent of women will be solely responsible for their finances and purchases at some point in their adult life. Factors that contribute to this not-so-surprising trend include a high divorce rate, more women choosing not to marry and women's longer life expectancy (widows outlive their mates by an average of seven years). Along with their growing income, women simply have more years to influence the economy.

TITLE IX INFLUENCES GENDER EQUITY

Passed in 1972, Title IX was landmark legislation that banned gender discrimination in athletics and that continues to create opportunities for women that their moms and grandmothers never had. In the thirty years since Congress approved this gender-equity law, sports leagues for girls and young women have become increasingly popular at all levels.

Interestingly, an April 2002 article in the *Chicago Tribune* reported that a study linked sports participation with success among women executives. "For women, the road to the boardroom may well lead through the locker room," concluded a survey of 401 women executives conducted by Oppenheimer Funds and its parent company, MassMutual Financial Group. "From the Locker Room to the Boardroom: A Survey on Sports in the Lives of Women Business Executives" provided food for thought, by showing the correlation between women playing sports in their early years (whether on cross-gender or all-girl teams) and their developing a sense of equality with their peers and a spirit of competition, which led to business successes in later years. Volleyball, soccer, basketball and any other school sport certainly do teach the values of discipline, teamwork and working toward a goal—so the connection to success in business makes good sense.

3. Run Your Numbers

Women today comprise a significant majority of customers for most businesses. So, focusing on their preferences is literally big business that can dramatically affect a company's sales, market share and profits.

So what's the point of going into the societal and historic changes that affected women's earning and spending power? It's to prove that the profile of your target market is ever changing (and evergreen) and to convince you to carry out the research (and expend the budget) to find out who is really buying your product or service, and why.

Women's buying power has snuck up on many companies that have historically considered men as their primary market. More than ever before, companies need to run their own numbers to get a solid idea of who actually influences the purchasing of their particular products and, finally, who carries out the cash-register transaction.

According to the manager of one credit union, with 93,000 members and annual revenue of $1 billion, surveying its member base every three years was well worth the continual effort. The results were always the same until the year 2000, when the typical member changed dramatically from a 53-year-old family man to a 46-year-old single workingwoman.

In his booklet *Women Roar,* marketing guru Tom Peters gives another striking example of a traditionally male-oriented company waking up to the shift in the gender of its core consumer: After some internal research, an owner of a company that produced and sold riding lawn mowers was shocked to discover that 80 percent of the customers who purchased his products were women, not men.

Given this swing over the past few decades in monetary power from men to women, many companies are still playing catch-up. If this applies to you, this book will help you make the quantum leap in refocusing your marketing efforts on your women customers.

BRAND-SPECIFIC AND COMPANY-FRIENDLY NUMBERS

When presenting your numbers and making your case about changing your company's approach to its customers, remember the importance of having strong research based on facts, not on opinions or assumptions. Keep in mind that you may need to customize your data in order for it to have an impact on your colleagues. Many people trust only data generated by their own people or that is specific to their own industry and brand. In addition, your marketers and salespeople probably need to see the size of the opportunity in a format they are accustomed to, or it won't help your case at all.

Thus, it is important to try putting the women's market opportunity in a familiar format, preferably using in-house data that is split by gender. If your team members are used to numbers and statistics, give them that; but if they respond better to bar graphs, use that imagery. We realize that even with your own data it can be a challenge to track the real economic influence of your female consumers. How often, for example, are women customers carrying out the prepurchase research and then making the purchase, but using their husband's credit card or account name? In general, we suggest reframing statistics to be as relevant as possible to your own brand, and translating the macro-level research into specific strategic observations and action points for your company.

4. Mainstream and Integrate Your Marketing to Women

Spread the knowledge about women's preferences and buying behaviors throughout your organization, rather than limiting yourself to an isolated women-focused marketing department. Yes, you read that right. Just say *no* to the entire concept of "women's initiatives." Women as a group are not a tidy niche. In fact, women constitute a huge market that can be segmented in many different ways. For most companies today, women and their varied buying behaviors are *the* market that can effectively make or break their brand.

A good example of a well-integrated organization is consumer packaged goods company Procter & Gamble. P&G has long been aware that women are its primary customers, and it is leading the industry in innovatively tailoring to women its sampling programs, Web sites and new product designs.

In contrast, historically male-focused industries like financial services, health care and automobile manufacturing may still be scrambling to identify the best methods for integrating their focus on women throughout their organizations. A good example of an effort in this direction is the work of Debra Nichols, senior vice president of Wachovia's women's financial advisory service. Nichols continually audits all the company's departments to assess how well they're connecting with and serving women and how they can improve their efforts. Nichols's executive-level position, backed by the full support and commitment of Wachovia's top leadership, helps ensure that all departments take her division seriously and embrace the company-wide commitment to reach women customers more effectively.

Given her experience in a large, traditionally male-focused industry, Nichols encourages other companies to include the women's angle in their existing objectives, rather than adding a separate business unit to market to women. "There is always an issue when trying to get separate funding for a new women's initiative. I personally struggle with the math to justify it, which is why we use the model that we do," she says, adding that with their system implementation costs are not incremental, but integral, to their overall budgets.[14]

While Wachovia's system has worked well for them, some in the financial services industries have tried this approach with less success because they lacked crucial internal support. In addition, some found that their lack of executive title, budget and staff made them less powerful and effective. These are important factors to consider as companies map out their internal strategies and approaches.

It will be important to continually observe and learn from the best practices of both consumer packaged goods and more traditionally male-focused industries as they shift their marketing focus and dollars onto their women customers.

5. Reframe Your Approach

Things have changed. It is true that once upon a time Caucasian males earned the bulk of the nation's income and made most of the decisions about how to spend it. As a result, most sales campaigns were designed and executed with men in mind. It made as much marketing sense then to follow the money as it does today.

So, how exactly does a company begin today to reframe its approach in order to appeal to women?

Early efforts to reach women were sincere but often lacked the right tone. These campaigns could affectionately be categorized as "pink," as they translated products, services and marketing materials into feminine or flowery versions of the original. Driven by stereotypes (pastel colors, overly sentimental copy, unrelatable characters and storylines), these early marketing efforts underperformed because they lacked depth of knowledge of what women customers really wanted. According to Vanessa Freytag, president of W-Insight Inc., a Cincinnati-based marketing firm that focuses on women, "Too many companies market to women unsuccessfully and then assume it a not a productive market rather than looking at the fact that *how* they did it might have been the problem."[15]

It is safe to say these ineffective albeit sincere pink campaigns have instilled a significant fear in the hearts of CEOs, marketers and employees about trying this women-focused thing themselves. In response to the failure of pink campaigns, a gender-neutral approach has arisen, wherein companies conclude that men and women are really not that different from each other—and even if they were, they wouldn't want to be marketed to differently. The gender-neutral marketing contingent feels that campaigns for women are insulting to the people they are trying to reach, and that they also turn off men at the same time.

As you can see, framing a campaign or product launch is probably one of the most confusing and least studied aspects of marketing to women. If you don't want to do a pink campaign yet are convinced that women do want an approach more tailored to their needs, what are your options? We propose a set of approaches that marketers might consider as they evaluate their market: visible, transparent and hybrid.

VISIBLE CAMPAIGNS

Some products just demand language and imagery that is unquestionably directed toward women. A few examples of successful visible campaigns include that of the Venus razor by The Gillette Company, or the way Wachovia created an online retirement calculator for women that factored in their longer lives and years outside the workforce. In the next chapter, we discuss how and when visible marketing to women works.

TRANSPARENT CAMPAIGNS

A subtle, yet more sophisticated, approach involves tailoring your message to meet women's needs without labeling the product or service exclusively for women. We call this "transparent marketing," a good example of which is the way Home Depot, Lowe's and other home improvement centers have started widening aisles (women like more room to browse and examine products on the lower shelves) and changing their offerings and displays to appeal to women's interests. While they do not label these efforts "for women" per se, their transparent campaigns differ from being gender neutral in that they acknowledge that women's preferences are different from men's. Home Depot and Lowe's follow transparent guidelines to more fully understand their customers and then develop full-service solutions, tailored services and products to attract a specific group of female do-it-yourselfers. As a bonus, by meeting the high expectations of women in a transparent fashion, they have noticed they are attracting more male customers as well.

There goes the theory that marketing to women is bound to alienate men.

Another example of transparent marketing done well comes from an unexpected source, the Entertainment and Sports Programming Network (ESPN). Clearly marketed to men, ESPN is pitch perfect with humor, tone, imagery and content. The multimedia giant delivers to the interests, preferences and priorities of men without labeling their magazine, TV and radio shows "ESPN sports for men." In chapter 3 we'll examine ESPN further and detail why we see transparency as the brightest future of good marketing to women.

HYBRID CAMPAIGNS

Thirdly, in a hybrid campaign, the overall marketing effort might remain transparent but certain products or elements are more visibly focused on women and their distinct needs. Home Depot's "Do it Herself" workshops promote a visible element within an overall transparent campaign. And, French Meadow Bakery, a Minneapolis-based company that has baked a line of ultrahealthy breads for years, recently introduced "Woman's Bread," featuring ingredients that specifically address women's health concerns. (Then, due to much demand, they quickly followed up with "Men's Bread.")

Home Depot and French Meadow Bakery both successfully reached out to women, in particular, by changing specific programs or redeveloping recipes, without repositioning their entire brand. You don't need to jump out on the sidewalk with a sandwich board that reads: "Women Shop Here. We Appreciate Women Customers!" Rather, by developing a product and marketing approach—visible, transparent or a hybrid mix of the two—along with delivering a customer experience that clearly demonstrates you know and value your female customers, you will be much more effective in reaching women.

6. Get Inside Her Mind

Men and women think differently. Science shows us that there are numerous biological, neurological and behavioral variations between the male and female brains. These gender differences range from how much information women take in and retain when they walk into a room, to their tendency to be more verbal and seek more human connections. When combined, these scientific differences, though sometimes small, can make a big difference in what attracts women to specific brands and makes them head to the checkout aisle.

When shopping, many women have a 360-degree perspective on life and evaluate products and services by how they fit into that bigger picture. More so than men, women are interactive in their shopping style and are more likely to try on, test and sample products before purchasing them; and they tend to imagine and envision how they will interact afterward with the products in their daily lives. Masters of tapping into people as resources, women interact more with sales associates and get more peer and expert opinions for their big-ticket purchases.

With its 24-7 convenience, the Internet has become a tool, a friend and an advisor for women in their daily lives and a time-saving advocate in their shopping. Women are using the Internet differently than their male peers, and in some cases women online even switch shopping styles with men—behaving in a more purpose-driven, "no time to browse" manner.

By understanding and responding to how women think and shop, marketers can begin to transparently tailor a shopping experience so that it seamlessly delivers on her preferences and eliminates time-gobbling friction (long lines, redundant forms, uninformed sales associates, lack of information). Research shows that companies that elevate their customer service practices based on women's higher standards not only deliver more intuitive shopping experiences, but increase their appeal and sales to both women and men.

In chapter 4 we will delve into the science underpinning a woman's mind and learn more about her buying behavior. Chapters 9 and 10 further illuminate women's online behavior and provide best practices and specific ways to more effectively use this medium to support the sale of your products.

7. Segment and Focus to Reveal Lucrative Markets

Never in history have American women been shaped by such a diverse set of experiences in the workplace. Today's female consumers are a mix of women with various viewpoints and life experiences. First, there exists a generation of women who grew up prior to the mass exodus away from home. Then, the Baby Boomer generation helped pave the way in the workforce (often at great personal and social expense). Finally, newer generations of women are expanding on these hard-won freedoms of work and career choices.

Each of these women has different perspectives. Even within these generations, there are subsets emerging everyday; for example, career women who decide to stay home and raise children; young women who opt not to marry and have a lot of disposable income; or unmarried women who decide to adopt children and raise them while working.

Women's opportunities have expanded dramatically over the past fifty years, and the result is a large and powerful market with an incredibly broad range of preferences and attitudes. A woman's specific experiences at home, school and work can affect her confidence with technology and finances as well as her shopping behavior and spending patterns.

The tendency to look at the average income and spending of women as one big group can be misleading and often results in missing a wealth of lucrative growth segments. For example, a company specializing in managing private wealth may consider the average income for women in the United States a modest figure.[16] Except that, further segmentation would reveal that there is a highly affluent group of women who are a great fit for the company's services.

By further examining the confidence level of these affluent women, our fictional company might discern that nearly half of the women are tentative investors who are not being well served by traditional brokerage houses. This information would lay the foundation for a much more tailored approach to their marketing to these affluent women.

Attitude and personal values are key segmenting factors that can also provide new (and often more effective) ways to focus on a market and to position products and services more effectively. For example, moms represent a significant niche for marketers. But the definition of a "mom" no longer refers only to women in their twenties and thirties with working husbands. The mom segment might include young, single mothers in their late teens or early twenties; college-educated women in their early thirties; fully employed women with fully employed husbands; or moms in their early forties who waited longer to start their families. Research has shown that the parenting style of mothers is often the most effective way to segment that group.

In Chapters 5 through 9 we will jump-start your segmentation efforts and, we hope, save you hundreds of hours and thousands of dollars in research. We will explore specific data and describe how to make it actionable in relating it to the shaping of generations, life stages and roles, emerging majorities, the confidence question and life transitions.

8. Try New Ways of Listening to Women

While the question of "what women want" is still humorously referred to as the eternal mystery, women can be amazing marketing partners who have an uncanny ability to articulate how a product or service might work better for them. Involving women customers earlier and more fully in the development process can help make your products and services far more compelling, long before they hit the market. Women in casual conversations have the power to help companies solve brand challenges, design more intuitive and relevant products, and create advertising messages that resonate—with humor and common sense that fit your trademark brand.

The antiquated methods of research that many retailers use to determine what their customers want may well be the critical disconnect between the seller and their mostly female buyers. According to Mary Lou Quinlan, CEO of Just Ask a Woman and a leading marketing consultant specializing in women consumers, "It isn't that retailers don't try to listen, but they're listening to 2003 women in 1950s ways. They do focus groups or surveys, but it's always something with a moderator in the middle that makes the consumer feel as if she's an experiment. The quickest way a retailer can find out what a woman wants is to stand next to the cash register or listen over the door to the fitting room, something that's face-to-face. You'll end up hearing a rundown of what's going on in their lives and what's not going on in your store."[17]

The Internet has also opened up the conversations with women and provided new ways to hear from them directly, using e-mail, tailored quizzes and online discussions. Because online responses are easily accessible, and because it is fairly simple to measure behavior and responses, the Internet can readily provide a wealth of information and insight for marketers.

The biggest advances in connecting with their women customers come when companies enlist them as their marketing partners and create an ongoing dialogue, whether live or in real time online. That's when listening and research truly become powerful and profitable.

9. Build In Ways to Measure Return on Investment

It is critical to build into your marketing programs ways to measure your return on investment (ROI). Often, focusing on women represents a new commitment for a company, and measuring ROI is a credible way to support your business case for increased budgets, staffing power and programming tailored to women's preferences. But, be aware that campaigns and programs targeted to women are frequently expected to produce results far different from comparable programs within the company!

Some marketing programs geared to women are mistakenly measured as if they were sales programs. In reality, your company's efforts in marketing to women should be treated like the rollout of any new service or product. If the process is incomplete and does not go through all the usual tests and procedural steps, it is illogical to expect the program to be successful or to yield the same results as a fully developed initiative.

That said, you should strive to build both traditional and innovative ways into your campaign in order to measure results and strengthen your business case. If possible, measure important indicators such as referrals, word of mouth and customer longevity, because those are the areas where the power of women customers as your marketing partners will have the most effect. Because a transparent approach will increase your appeal to all customers, be sure to also measure new male customers and the increased spending from men as well.

Let's consider the experience of Wachovia's Debra Nichols again. She created an award-winning "Women's Financial Center" as part of Wachovia's main Web site, which included a dedicated e-mail address (not just a general Wachovia information address) and dedicated 800 numbers. Then, Nichols carefully analyzed the quality and type of calls and e-mails the center received through those channels. She discovered that fully 50 percent of the e-mail correspondence to Wachovia's Women's Financial Center included buying questions that indicated highly qualified prospects! The center received a dramatically higher percentage of qualified prospects than did any other part of the company's Web site and showed a strong return on investment.

In another example, Patti Ross, segment executive of women-owned businesses at IBM, began populating the company database with female small business owners, which led to more accurately measuring women's sales activity against those of the general small business customer—a simple database adjustment with big measurement and market research results.

10. Carpe Diem

When we first started consulting on marketing to women, we almost had to convince prospective clients of the overwhelming and exciting opportunity in connecting with women. We are happy to report that in the past few years there has been a steady, though gradual, growth of marketing efforts focused on reaching women.

"Marketing to women is still something of a frontier, an extreme sport, if you will," reported Lisa Finn, editor of EPM

Communications' newsletter, *Marketing to Women,* based on a November 2002 subscriber survey. The survey pointed to an increasing interest in the women's market, and that "almost a third (31 percent) report that the numbers of people in their organizations who work on women's marketing have increased in the past two years, while 56 percent say the number has stayed the same."[18]

It can be fairly scary to make a bold, wholesale commitment to a market where few seem to know the new rules. In many cases companies genuinely want to respond to women's needs, but their tentative testing of the waters is based on the hope that a small change will suffice, and that a more in-depth change with bigger budgets won't have to be pursued. It's a hopeful, quick-fix attitude, and we can understand it.

Certainly, everyone wants a simple solution so they can feel productive and get on with their lengthy list of to dos. But in the case of marketing to women, these cursory efforts are like piling up sandbags against a hundred-year flood—hoping against hope that a small amount of preparation will hold and do the job.

More than anything, this shift in women's marketing away from pink thinking is your company's opportunity to gain a competitive advantage and spur growth. An assessment of the marketplace shows that most companies are still trying to figure out how they will respond internally, so now is the time to pioneer and lead the charge! This book is about equipping companies and marketers with the tools to go beyond thinking pink and to start serving a bigger slice of today's largest market segment—women.

CHAPTER 2

now you see "her"

the visible approach
to marketing to women

THE TWO MAIN methods for reaching consumers of either gender we call the "visible" and "transparent" approaches to marketing—plus a third or "hybrid" approach that combines the two. Each of these options can be highly effective in reaching women in particular. The success of one approach or another depends on the product or service, the profiles of your core women customers, and the ways in which they want to be reached.

In some cases, it makes a lot of sense to adopt the visible approach, distinguishing your product from the many others on the shelf by directly calling out "for women." In other cases, the best way to resonate with women requires marketing to them transparently—by delivering the product or service in a way that works with women's information gathering and purchasing processes, but that doesn't single them out as a special group.

Finally, the third marketing option connects with your female customers in a hybrid way through a combination of the two approaches, which usually means calling out "for women" or creating a special women's initiative for a particular product or service within an existing brand.

You just can't avoid wrestling with the decision about how to best reach the women in your market. There's much to consider, as we show throughout this book's exploration of a woman's buying mind and what influences it. What we do know is that your brand must do all it can to align itself with its female consumers' existing perspective of your product or service. Only by meeting women where they are, can you gain their trust and then be able to give them a new view of your wares.

In this chapter, we explore the visible approach, in particular; and we also touch on how you can include more visible elements when marketing to women within a traditional marketing campaign, resulting in a hybrid approach. Though we suspect that in coming years there will be fewer occasions to effectively utilize the visible option, it's certainly worth touching upon. Your marketing brain should be aware of all the choices, so you can make the best decisions for connecting with your women customers.

"For Women" Only

Visible campaigns are clearly designed and presented "for women." There will be no question. Such a gender-specific focus may jump right out at you in the name of the product, like French Meadow Bakery's "Woman's Bread"; or it may be clearly a women's-only product like a health supplement for menopausal symptoms (there's just no avoiding that specificity).

Well executed, a visible approach can streamline the way to women's buying minds and deliver a truly customized brand experience. The most successful current "for women" approaches may be those for female-specific nutrition, body care and beauty products. Just think of the "women's formula" statements on the packages of nutritional supplements, or consider the Gillette Venus razor campaign, as examples of effective visible marketing to women.

Stamping "women's formula" on your vitamin bottle will help guide women to the shelves reserved for "women's wellness" offerings at drug and grocery stores. Still, with media coverage of nutrition and diet increasing in the past ten or so years, women are that much more likely to have already read up on the nutritional needs for their particular life stage. These well-informed consumers will be very conscious of including the appropriate elements in their diet, so they'll love the extra guidance they find at the grocery store shelf.

And then there are the newer shapes of women's razors that do speak, purposefully, "for women." There is just something about giving a razor a new, more feminine curvy shape and pastel color that means so much to women who've been using their husband's disposables for years.

In the case of Gillette's Venus razor for women, even before naming it and thus making the marketing campaign visible, the product would still have resonated with women. Without the girly name, the Venus' marketing approach would have been more transparent, because the color and shape of the product—and its improved ability to maneuver in the usually hard-to-reach areas on a woman's body—still tell the story on their own. Whether the marketing approach is visible or transparent, women everywhere applaud razor manufacturers who have became cognizant of the many curves and odd angles women encounter when they shave—and that, on its own, reflects a greater awareness of women's buying mind and consumer needs.

visibly marketing nutrition for women

Whatever the product, from a breakfast cereal to a power bar, there is now a massive market for specific products that meet gender-unique nutritional needs.

The brands that entered the nutrition-for-women market likely based their decisions on U.S. Department of Agriculture (USDA) findings, like those from 1996: Less than half of all women ingest the recommended levels of vital nutrients, such as calcium and iron.

It has by now been well documented that diet plays a big role in the prevention of osteoporosis, heart disease and cancer. Then, too, accommodating women's busy lives has further impelled the development of quick ways to fit solid nutrition into a woman's daily routine. By talking with women early on in the development of a nutritional product, you'd likely understand the best way to customize the product and packaging to zero in on women's concerns. Changes might include:

▫ Provide a good portion of each day's calcium requirement to prevent osteoporosis.

▫ Add nutrients and soy protein to boost protection against heart disease.

▫ Use promotional copy that espouses the product's essential nutrients specifically for a woman's diet.

▫ Maintain your established logo and brand, but possibly include a female graphic element.

▫ Package the product to reflect a woman's mobile life, for example, in individually wrapped portions or smaller containers (environmental concerns aside).

As women's health has gotten more and more coverage across all media channels over the years, few women have escaped the realization that they have unique nutritional needs. Creating a product branded "for women" that provides key gender-specific nutritional elements utilizes a visible approach to its utmost beneficial effect. Making it easy for a woman to learn about and find your product through visible ad campaigns, package design, shelf placement and product naming will further enhance your sales.

In specific cases, women embrace those brands that were developed to meet their gender-specific needs, highlighting "for women" or "for her" in their title and packaging.

The Hybrid Approach: Specifying "For Her" Within an Established Brand

There are those cases in which a new product or service line, created within an established overall brand, would benefit from calling out to women that it was developed specifically for them. Consider your local well-known bank as an example. Everyone knows "Downtown Bank" has good customer service, offering the best interest rates with free checking; but now Downtown wants to package its information and develop seminars specifically to address women's financial needs. The bank certainly wouldn't redo its logo or reposition itself to become "Women's Downtown Bank." Rather, it may develop a Web site section called "Financial Services for Women" and start offering "for women" seminars on financial planning for retirement and on gender-specific issues, such as earning less but living longer than one's male spouse.

Drugstore.com's "Healthy Woman" area is effectively women-specific within a well-known brand. The section includes products and information on both traditional and alternative approaches to women's health, as well as a resource section, called a "Health Guide," that carries the woman-resonant tagline "knowledge is power." Items are presented in categories that speak directly to women's prime concerns, like cardio and breast health. Healthy Woman's top ten solutions for weight loss, antiaging and more appear front and center on the home page. By delivering the products and information in ways that serve so well the buying minds of women, this visible "for women" approach within the Drugstore.com brand is getting full power from its marketing efforts.

Rejuvenating Effects toothpaste is another product representative of the hybrid approach to marketing to women. Developed as a product within Procter & Gamble's Crest line, it is promoted as the first toothpaste targeted specifically to women using the slogan, "For a radiant smile, today's new beauty secret."

In keeping with a hybrid approach, the entire Crest brand was not given a "for women" makeover. Rather, the Rejuvenating Effects product within the Crest brand is being distinctly marketed as a toothpaste that addresses a beauty concern, which is usually female-specific.

Interestingly, while Drugstore.com's Healthy Woman area packages and categorizes information and products specifically around women's health concerns, Rejuvenating Effects toothpaste is more simply positioned "for women" without containing any truly female-specific ingredients.

A hybrid marketing approach may be a great way to test whether women are paying attention to your brand. If they do notice and respond to your visible efforts to reach them, then that may be the time to develop and launch an even more powerful transparent marketing program (see the next chapter for details).

Reality-Based Visibility

When a visible approach, either on its own or as part of a hybrid program, reinforces outdated stereotypes of women and their preferences for the sake of a marketing pitch, it will turn off both women and men alike. Talk about backfiring!

From our own conversations with women over the years, we can report that many feel an almost physical discomfort in response to a marketing effort that discounts them, pegs them as "typical" women, or mistakenly or superficially uses flowers and pastels to reach them. There are so many more exciting ways to reach women.

A good thing to consider, when assessing the value of a visible campaign for reaching your market, is how connected to a woman's specific realities (body size, shape and health) your product or service may be, and how her emotions around those topics may affect her purchase. For example, golf clubs reengineered for a woman's smaller grip, swing and size, or specialized bike seats for women, are cases where a visible approach is the best choice.

When products like golf clubs or bike seats present an innovation for women, in an industry where the standard has been shorter or smaller versions of the men's line, a visible, women-specific campaign helps highlight the change. Your brand's new attention to a woman's specific needs for designs and features will positively influence her view of your overall brand, and guide her toward just what she seeks.

Creating visible campaigns without a strong purpose, however, can be risky. Running into a "for women" approach while shopping for a lawnmower or a PDA, for example, might feel demeaning to many. (What, the lawnmower is purple and thus built specifically "for women"?) A woman's buying mind doesn't signal that such superficially modified products are gender-specific, so a visible marketing approach would be only distracting, at best, counterproductive, at worst.

Yet, there are ways to develop and market those lawnmowers, PDAs and home electronics that will make them more loudly resonate with women and help them to be seen more clearly through a woman's buying perspective. We call that invisible approach "transparent," and will go into that more in the pages to come.

Generational Cues

Previous generations of women may have responded more readily to visible, or "for her," marketing efforts, because they were novel and seemed to represent a new sense of respect for gender differences. However, younger generations have now grown up in more gender-neutral worlds and so are less likely overall to respond to that approach to marketing to women.

Oatmeal for women? Whatever. Why do I need my own oatmeal? For some reason this approach really turns me off. But you know who would buy this? My mom!

—Lori T., age 28, advertising account manager

The one caveat in marketing to the younger generation is that they can always turn a stereotype on its ear and play against it just for fun. In the early 2000s, the retail marketplace went through a "pink" and "girly" craze, of sorts, in clothing, gadgets and other nonessential products geared toward younger women. This trend was almost a sophisticated embracing of the stereotypes, a sort of "wink-wink, nudge-nudge" way of responding with humor and sass to the age-old paradigm that women love things pink, feminine and flowery.

Furthermore, while some Mature generation women and even some Baby Boom women may not have previously been offended by visible campaigns, the tide may be turning. These older women's exposure to marketing messages over the years has surely made them more discriminating consumers. And, there is nothing like too-quickly adding "for women" to a product's name, or painting its package pink, to make your marketing motives suspect.

Integrating Visibility

Quality, price and reputation will mean nothing if a woman can tell you slapped a "for women" sticker on the pastel version of the same old product. If you haven't developed truly gender-specific features and benefits, or conducted research into how a woman might buy the product, it will be evident to your potential customers. To keep your products and marketing authentic and integrated, you should decide whether to use the visible approach right from the beginning. Let product development in response to women's real needs dictate your sales efforts and marketing messages.

For example, if the Gillette Venus razor had not been designed specifically for a woman's body, its more feminine color and name would feel inauthentic to potential buyers, and Gillette's visible approach would have failed. As it is, the shape of the razor was designed intentionally to fit a woman's curves, so the color and name integrated well with the design and thus felt authentic.

A woman's interest in purchasing your product or service will be significantly affected by whether your brand's marketing approach is genuine, through and through, or a superficial (however sincere) effort to gain her attention. So, choose and utilize the visible marketing option with great care if you want to reach women.

Companies certainly don't set out to make products that will fail with women. Success comes by making the effort to understand the women customers you are trying to reach before you even create the product. Then, a genuine reality-based visible approach can win new customers and create new markets.

CHAPTER 3

now you don't (see "her")

the transparent approach to marketing to women

WHILE VISIBLE marketing certainly tells women that a specific product or service is for them (often to mixed reviews), transparently connecting with women requires a much more sophisticated method built on in-depth knowledge of your market, innovative solutions to the specific challenges of your customers and inspired choices reflecting those women's preferences. It takes more work, but transparency attracts your market, builds brand loyalty and increases sales in a way that a visible campaign can't.

Transparent marketing requires companies to go beyond making obvious and stereotype-driven changes, to truly tailoring their brands for specific markets. These programs fit women's lifestyles and reflect women's priorities in subtle and surprising ways. When you have obviously gathered information about your key women customers, and learned how and why they buy products or services like yours, women will see the relevance of your brand.

The Tale of the Tailored Suit

Have you ever chosen a business suit off the rack and felt that the fit was just somehow off? You'll recognize the experience: The label read your size, but the shoulders drooped slightly, the hips flared unattractively and the back was too full, making you look ten pounds heavier. Initially you might have thought, "I look like a cow in a suit," or just conclude that you should never shop right after lunch. But, if you were lucky (or at Nordstrom!), a sales associate quickly came to the rescue and sent in a tailor who started pinning and tucking. Within moments, the nips and tucks made you look sleeker, slimmer and more professional in that suit. The changes made the suit fit your shape like a glove, and that retailer (and that tailor) became your new best friend.

Why go into this suit story? Because, transparently reaching women is the equivalent of delivering an inspired, custom-tailored product and marketing strategy instead of a visible, off-the-rack, "for women" marketing campaign.

Believe us, women notice and invest in brands that take the time to take their measurements correctly and learn how they live and how they use the product. Custom-tailored, transparently fitted campaigns are the path to long-term brand loyalty and multiple purchases.

Transparency Is the Future

As general awareness of the economic power of women increases, and as the younger generations of women wield more influence in the marketplace, we predict that transparent positioning will become the rule, while visible campaigns will be the exception.

When your brand commits the time and effort to develop products and marketing tactics that serve and reach your female customers most effectively, a transparent campaign results. And, it will likely be received as well as a newly tailored suit. Your female customers will notice you paid attention to their preferences, and you won't need a "for women" tagline to call them out or get their attention.

Transparent marketing is really just good marketing. Using a transparent approach will not only help companies serve the high expectations of their women customers, but in many cases it will help them increase market share with men as well. The exponential result is part of why we see transparency as the future of all great marketing efforts to women.

From the style of information you deliver to the ease of use of your products, the things that resonate with your female customers should be seamlessly embedded into the buying process, providing a streamlined and frictionless shopping experience.

Doing that, your Web site will seem to serve your customers well and attend to their buying needs. Your customers might not fathom why it took you so long to develop, but your brand finally did it—the perfect breakfast solution for their kids, for example! And, you didn't have to slap "for women" or "for moms" on the package!

Even though I'd like to have the willpower to buy books solely through my local independent bookstore, I keep finding myself heading to Amazon.com. It's like a drug. I love that I can compile a wish list, or easily build up my shopping cart and wait until there's enough in it to get free shipping. And, I'm a total sucker for their recommendations and the reviews by people who've already read the book or bought the CD.

—Ann H. , age 37, business journalist

The more sophisticated and relevant ways that a transparent approach meets customer needs make it so effective for reaching women. By tapping into their actual buying needs and preferences, your brand demonstrates its awareness of women and its value for them as customers. Calling out to women with "for women" products and programs is annoying to many (especially the younger set), and can even make a new product look dated or less sophisticated.

What's more, in many cases when you market transparently, men will likely also come to realize that they prefer shopping on your site or at your store, because of some indescribable sense they get in dealing with your staff and products. In general, customers may say things like, "It just seems friendly." Or, "Their site is so intuitive, I can get my shopping done quickly." Or, "They make returns so easy and they offer all the products I love."

By doing your homework, you've smoothed the way for fast, efficient and comfortable purchasing experiences for your customers. There is nothing gender-biased about that.

The Keys to Transparent Marketing

Transparently reaching women is all about making great changes in your product and marketing that are inspired by women, but appreciated by everyone. The heart of the matter is providing solutions— and an industry's gold standard will be those that are intuitive and take the hassle out of buying. A woman's response to your transparent ways will inspire her to rave to friends, "Why didn't I think of that?" Or, "I can't imagine doing it any other way."

Transparent marketing involves a lot more preparatory research and connecting with your women's market than a visible effort might. Here are a few keys to developing an effective and resonant transparent campaign from the start:

1. NARROW YOUR FOCUS. No matter how much you want to, you won't be able to market all at once toward a broad spectrum of ages, life stages or cultures. The more mass appeal you create, the more likely your message will become too diluted to appeal to just those women with whom you need to be relevant. So, force yourself to decide upon those women who will likely be the early adopters of, or best fit for, your product or service. If you start with that narrowly defined but important group, their passion for your brand will attract a wider audience.

A good example of this in action is the yoga fitness movement. The culture and lifestyle around yoga, which originally served quite a narrow niche, are now embraced by a much broader market. The small passionate core group of early practitioners demonstrated the benefits of these health practices and commitments. Now celebrities and aging Boomers are taking it mainstream. Suddenly the yoga culture is fueling the new designs of workout clothes and shoes, the increasing adoption of eastern-inspired religions and practices, and a new awareness and passion for organic and raw food diets.

2. UNDERSTAND THE CUSTOMER COMMUNITY INTIMATELY. You've identified that powerful community of focus, so now it is essential to understand what influences it. Two important things to consider as you explore the wants and needs of these women:

A day in their life. Do what you can to learn about their daily routines, common thoughts and regular stresses. What are their motivations and what are their fears? What pushes their buttons? How do things work within their community? What music do they listen to?

These are some intimate, touchy-feely questions to pose. But this is how you dig deep to retrieve the cues you need in order to form your transparent strategies. Only when you know these fine details of the lives of those women with whom you'd like to build brand loyalty, can you see how your products, services and messages will fit their needs and their ways of learning about things.

A day in their dreams. Shared hopes, desires and belief structures, even more than generational commonalities, bring women together in community and define the boundaries of market segments. For instance, a commitment to organic gardening and an aspiration to protect the environment long-term are both examples of beliefs that can transcend all generations, cultures and life stages.

3. BUILD CUSTOMER FEEDBACK INTO YOUR PROCESS. Go beyond just understanding your market to involving your customers and marketing *with* them. Instead of getting feedback about a product or program once it is virtually on the shelf (too little input, too late), include women sooner and more often when building something new.

4. FOCUS ON YOUR PRODUCT'S CONTEXT. Design your customer experience around those key scenarios or life stages that occur in the community of women on which your brand is focused. Consider how your brand might be positioned to turn up in the doctor's waiting room, in the store aisle or in the mailbox, just as your customer thinks about or needs your product or service.

> ## defining questions of a transparent brand
>
> *Does your brand have personality?* Brand personality can come from the sassiness of your ad copy or the voice-over style of your radio ads or even from the founder of your company— like Suze Orman, who has become her own brand of financial awareness.
>
> Politically correct does not equal a brand personality. There seems to be a myth that the best way to draw more women into a brand is to make it more universal, but this often results in a more bland, tasteless personality. Instead, the

marketplace is rewarding brands with more fully developed (even spicy) personalities. You really see this with Gen Yers who have turned up their noses at many of the industry giants (think of how Levi's has been scrambling these past years) to pursue smaller brands with quirks, sass and attitude. If you want to reach more women, introduce their favorite flavors instead of turning everything to vanilla.

It is also important to note that a brand doesn't necessarily need to have a feminine personality to appeal to women. Some brands are attractive to women because of their more masculine personality. We can think of specific tools, movies, tire stores and liquor brands that have a huge appeal to women which would diminish if they were more feminized. That doesn't mean that those brands shouldn't target women in their media buying and in customizing their service according to her high standards. But they certainly don't need to inject any estrogen into their brand personality to be more appealing to their women customers.

What is your brand's language? The language your brand uses is both an element of brand personality, as discussed above, and also a stand-alone concern. Whether your brand seems to present a more masculine or more a feminine "feel"; whether its design standards employ soft colors and short paragraphs or dark colors and dense text; to whether the copy takes a formal tone or expresses a lot of humor—there will be many elements and nuances to the marketing dialect you've built over time. All these things need to be integrated to reflect a language that can be heard and understood by your women's market.

Does your brand's language include the voice of a company founder, an industry expert or a key customer? For example, Suze Orman delivers her financial advice in a voice that always seems to come directly from her. In a less obvious example, the sports network ESPN has worked to develop multiple personalities that give voice to their wide range of content. Some companies use animated and drawn characters to lend personality to their brands, such as "Snap, Crackle and Pop," who bring Kellogg's Rice Krispies cereal alive.

5. UNDERSTAND AND DEFINE YOUR BRAND. Let your brand's spirit step forward, instead of diluting it in an attempt to be everything to everyone. The danger these days in building a marketing effort to women isn't so much about being politically correct, it's more about the hazards of becoming too similar to the bland campaigns of other brands. When you know what sets your brand apart and effectively present and promote that uniqueness, you'll more likely capture the attention of women and get the buzz started with their friends.

6. BE AUTHENTIC. Share your brand's attitude and honestly reveal both its strengths and weaknesses. The community you are trying to reach will appreciate such forthrightness, and that will also help them gain trust in the people behind the brand.

"why didn't I think of that?" ten products or services that reflect transparent marketing

Ford Windstar: Developed a dimmer switch on the overhead interior light, so sleeping kids could be transported home without being awakened by the bright light.

Wal-Mart: Created an atmosphere of immediate welcome by coming up with the idea for store greeters.

Starbucks: Features cozy chairs for lingering and offers wireless access for an office away from the office.

Bliss Spa: Staff members send patrons handwritten thank-you notes.

Les Schwab: Salespeople run out to your car to greet you and will repair your tires for free.

Sephora: Purposefully displays its selections in an accessible and inviting way and has a high number of staff on the retail floor, so women can easily test lipsticks, blush and skin care products, and feel free to ask questions.

Reflect.com: Invites you to develop and customize your own lotions and cosmetics, right down to choosing a name and picking the packaging.

Saturn: Introduced the no-dicker sticker price to appeal to women auto buyers.

TiVo: Brought television viewing back under a mother's control (among other features). Now you could record every episode of *SpongeBob SquarePants* and allow your kids to watch the show at *your* convenience.

Terry Precision Cycling: Introduced the now-famed women-specific bicycle saddle (it's the one with the hole in it), and then developed one for men as well.

What Transparent Marketing Looks Like: Brought to You by ESPN!

Sometimes the easiest way to understand a new concept is to look at it from a completely different angle. One of the best examples we've found to demonstrate effective transparency as well as good visible marketing is the Entertainment and Sports Programming Network (ESPN) brand—and yes, we know, it traditionally serves men. But, bear with us.

ESPN's hip sports empire includes 24-hour cable networks, a Web site, a radio network, a print magazine and theme restaurants. This fast-growing, multichannel media brand brilliantly and transparently targets young, affluent male sports fans. The entire ESPN brand focuses on delivering pitch-perfect content to their target demographic, men, and in so doing has gained the affection and respect of many male and female sports fans alike. Because they are not *trying* to be all things to all customers, they can dig deep into the humor, preferences and interests of their male market.

Before we examine the specific elements of ESPN's successful transparent marketing approach, we'll paint a picture of what it would look like if ESPN visibly marketed its magazine to men in the way many women's brands do. Let's look at an *ESPN: The Magazine* painted male blue:

ESPN: THE MAGAZINE WITH VISIBLE MARKETING

- The tagline would be "A magazine for male sports enthusiasts."

- The staff would be all male; the photos would all depict men; and the articles would cover only men's teams.

- Columns like these would be included: "A Man's Perspective on . . . ," covering sports industry issues; and "His Turn," espousing a male viewpoint on topics typically covered by women.

- Photos would show the usual: a collection of men from a variety of nationalities, each wearing their team uniforms and holding the appropriate sporting goods or equipment (a soccer ball, a hockey stick, for example).

- The stories and cartoons would feature the usual stereotypical male humor about beer bellies, couch potatoes, armchair quarterbacks and hot cheerleaders.

▫ Advertisers would sell traditional men's products using departments focused on reaching men.

▫ Specialized "for men" programs might include interactive tools such as the body fat calculator for men; the all-men's fantasy football league; the sports-savvy men's sports quiz; and the athletic men's guide to sports history.

▫ The magazine's palette would stick to clichéd, "male-appropriate" primary colors, with a strong emphasis on royal blue.

▫ The magazine would sponsor events around major male health concerns, like prostate cancer benefit runs or heart disease bowling tournaments.

▫ It would all be politically correct and professionally carried out, but not very inspiring.

Now doesn't it just seem bizarre to envision ESPN reaching men visibly in this way? Doesn't it wake you up a bit to how women customers might perceive the visible "for women" efforts that come their way?

Let's turn things right-side up and examine how ESPN is actually capturing an avid fan base of both men and women, with their sophisticated and fun transparent approach. Considering the essential elements of transparent marketing we cited earlier in this chapter, here's what ESPN does so well:

The ESPN Brand with Transparent Marketing

1. NARROW YOUR FOCUS. ESPN targets a narrow and devoted market of young, affluent, male sports fans. They don't even list women in the demographics page of their media kit. In keeping with the rules of transparent marketing, they focus on delivering to the preferences of their core market, but have also developed a passionate following from a broader base.

2. UNDERSTAND YOUR CUSTOMER COMMUNITY INTIMATELY. Remember that *bigger is better.* In size, paper stock and attitude, *ESPN: The Magazine* resembles *Spin* and *Vibe*, which have become editorial bibles for attracting a target audience of Gen X men. Also important:

Eye candy. The louder and hipper graphic layout of *ESPN: The Magazine* is a huge departure from the designs of competitive publications, and it reflects a keen understanding of their younger audience.

Large, vivid photographs. ESPN concluded that the best play action is shown on TV, in replays and slow-motion. You just can't beat what is shot live by minicams on a goalie's skates. Instead, *ESPN: The Magazine* developed an innovative photographic style that includes vivid portraits and multiple-page photo spreads to make the still shots as inspiring as the ESPN television offerings. Readers like the photographs so much they use the spreads as posters.

Extreme sports coverage. ESPN was the first major multimedia sports brand to give significant print and airtime coverage to extreme sports like surfing El Niño, snowboarding, BMX racing and wakeboarding.

3. BUILD CUSTOMER FEEDBACK INTO YOUR PROCESS. *Talk shows with back talk* such as ESPN's are one the strongest vehicles for maintaining an ongoing dialogue with fans. The daily radio shows encourage live phone calls from listeners and have developed a group of regular contributors who keep the show's phone number on speed dial. ESPN radio fans are eager to share their opinions and viewpoints in the same witty, brash and straightforward style of their favorite talk show hosts. E-mail is also used to weave listeners opinions into the live shows. For example, popular talk show host Jim Rome regularly taunts and invites the "clones" to respond to his opinions. This witty group of listeners e-mail taunting comments in real-time that Rome gleefully reads on his show.

4. FOCUS ON YOUR PRODUCT'S CONTEXT. ESPN is aware of its *information-hungry sports enthusiasts.* Knowing its members are passionate about their specific sports personalities and teams, ESPN offers both great coverage and a relatively cheap online service to check up on articles from around the country. The magazine also provides the countless stats, charts and graphs that are essential to hardcore sports fans. They are also aware of:

Year-round interest. For many fans the best part of *ESPN: The Magazine* may be that, regardless of the sport season, they'll have reports in every major sports category. Getting up-to-date news on baseball in December and on college football during July sets this magazine far apart from other leading sports publications.

Connections to fellow fans. The multimedia capabilities of ESPN mean that their on-air personalities for all sports can both contribute articles and participate in online chat sessions, giving fans a chance to interact with them and with each other. From fantasy-football software online to printable fill-in rosters for forecasting college basketball's "March Madness," ESPN equips fans with the resources and services needed to fuel the competitive fire in their local sports communities.

5. UNDERSTAND AND DEFINE YOUR BRAND. The ESPN SportsCenter has produced a variety of *distinct brand personalities* to whom ESPN fans respond with celebrity-obsessed devotion. Their on-air personalities, as mentioned above, get further personalized connection time with fans by contributing articles and participating in chat sessions. They also keep in mind such things as:

Humor. The ESPN SportsCenter is renowned for its style and humor. (The show even inspired the popular but short-lived 1999–2000 ABC sitcom, *Sports Night.*) For many fans, ESPN is more enjoyable because it doesn't always present the information in a serious manner and isn't afraid to have fun at the expense of the athletes, the fans and, most importantly, the sportscasters and on-air personalities themselves.

Insider's code. The ESPN SportsCenter has coined a quirky and fun sports language all its own that serves as an insider code to its devoted audience. Comments like "Boo-yah!"; "Fade. Fire. Fill."; "Dunk you very much" and "Get down with your bad self" unite sports fans everywhere.

Insider scoop. ESPN doesn't just ask the same old questions like, "Scottie, what was it like being traded from Chicago to Houston?" Their interviewers go deeper with questions like, "Scottie, have you ever just wanted to let Charles Barkley have it?" Or, "Aren't you tired of playing with Michael Jordan?" The audience gets the answers to questions they've always wanted to ask the sports figures themselves.

The "brand language" of *ESPN: The Magazine* includes short bursts of text and a fast-paced storytelling style (perfect for the attention span of their core readership). Their use of fun and hip titles for typical magazine departments, like "Zoom," "The Sports Guy," "Outtakes" and "0:01 (with the beloved Dick Vitale)" also significantly resonate with their reader demographic.

6. BE AUTHENTIC. Bold, irreverent and sometimes shocking, ESPN-brand sports coverage gives fans everywhere an honest and inside look into their favorite athletes and teams. Their no-holds-barred style conveys the feeling of an honest, authentic, appealing and savvy sports empire.

ESPN is a useful case study for marketers because it vividly demonstrates a core principle of transparent marketing: *If you know your customers intimately, you can use their core values, preferences and even quirks to both reflect back their personalities and define your brands.*

In addition, we have found it easier for many people to understand transparent marketing from the male perspective, because it clears away from the discussion all the politics and diversity issues. Seeing how a company focused on a single gender without drawing from tired stereotypes helps lift the pink fog that can surround this marketing concept.

Transparency in a Traditional Industry

ESPN is all well and good, as an example of transparent marketing, but you're thinking, "Seriously, it's a multimedia empire—and a much more creative endeavor—so of course their tactics can be much more transparent." So, to give you an example of a more traditionally run industry that needed help developing transparency to reach women, let's look at the home improvement category.

Prior to the industry's awakening, if you will, a customer would enter a big boxy warehouse store with row upon row of ceiling-high shelving. Plumbing was a separate section, as was electrical and wood. The typical salesperson could mostly handle only questions about the section where he or she had been planted. If you didn't know there were several types of pipes and tubing used in plumbing projects, you might leave the store with the totally wrong item.

Fade to the present. There are updated versions of Ace Hardware; and Home Depot and Lowe's both deliver more modern home improvement shopping experiences. Having woken up to the fact that women are now a major portion of their core customer demographic, home improvement stores are innovating each year.

Whether it's because more people these days are do-it-yourself (DIY) types, or whether there's a nesting trend, you can't help but notice that women as well as men are flocking to home improvement and hardware stores. How did the industry change its marketing, and how did the stores respond, in order to attract the attention and loyalty of so many women?

Let's look at the same transparent principles we examined in the ESPN case study.

The Home Improvement Industry Becomes Transparent

1. NARROW YOUR FOCUS. A growing body of research revealed to the home improvement industry that women (especially those with a do-it-yourself attitude) should be their focus. Here are a few examples of what convinced them to shift their marketing dollars onto women:

□ A 2003 survey by Lowe's found 80 percent of women are doing "everyday fix-it" projects around the house on their own.[1] According to Jim Rhodes, a Lowe's store manager, "It is no longer a male-dominated industry. Ninety-four percent of our shoppers who are females are do-it-yourselfers, and 80 percent of the females make the decisions when it comes to home improvement needs."[2]

□ According to a 2002 Ace Hardware's "America's To-Do List" study of one thousand homeowners, 62 percent of respondents said that the woman of the house is at least partially responsible for physically tackling home repairs and improvement projects.[3] The study also found that men spend an average of $12.27, while women spend an average of $17.74, each time they visit an Ace Hardware store.[4]

□ A 2003 survey by the Home Improvement Research Institute of Tampa, Florida, showed that women are getting involved in do-it-yourself projects at a faster rate than men are.[5] In fact, the number of do-it-yourself products purchased by men has declined over the last two years.[6]

2. UNDERSTAND YOUR CUSTOMER COMMUNITY INTIMATELY.
Forget *waiting for "honey" to fix it.* The real empowerment for
women doing home improvement projects results from the desire
not to have to wait for husbands or significant others to do the job.
"Honey to-do lists" are not so amusing to women who patiently
wait until weekends for projects to get started—and then often go
unfinished. Others experience frustration when something breaks
down and they can't find a handyman to fix it. More aware that
women are leading the home improvement charge, salespeople are
responding to them with higher levels of attention and customer
service. Also keep in mind:

Transparent tools. To avoid tipping the balance toward pink,
more manufacturers are developing transparently designed easier-
to-handle tools with improved features (such as no cords and more
comfortable grips) that have the same exterior design features as the
rest of their lines. RotoZip's lightweight power spiral saw, the Makita
"Impact Driver" and Black & Decker's "Mouse Sander" (a lightweight sander) are examples of transparently marketed tools developed to suit women's smaller hands and frames.

Innovative solutions. The home improvement industry is making
their old stand-by tools, products and packaging easier to use. For
example, Sherwin-Williams Dutch Boy brand paint with its
"Twist & Pour" square plastic containers is very consumer friendly.
Replacing that age-old purveyor of paint and frustration, the round
metal can, Dutch Boy's new packaging innovation features a twist
top, a built-in side handle and a no-drip spout. In another example,
hardwood- and laminate-floor manufacturers have reconceived the
design of their products to make them easier to install by the average layperson.

Brains over brawn. While men like many of the same new features
designed to appeal to women, there's still one key difference in the

tool world: the lust for megapower. An ad in an issue of *Builder* magazine features a brawny guy in a plaid shirt, brandishing a huge power saw:[7] "Fourteen houses and this . . . blade's still eatin' boards like it's day one," the copy brags. With this product, "the blades don't stop until you do." Owning and using power tools is empowering, but for many women the power comes from the ability to use the tools not the torque.

3. BUILD CUSTOMER FEEDBACK INTO YOUR PROCESS. It's important to *interact personally.* Classes and other methods of personally interacting with customers are a great way to gain feedback. Home Depot, Ace and Lowe's all offer do-it-yourself classes on everything from installing tile floors to faux painting. Women-only classes are becoming increasingly popular, as many women prefer to work in teams and learn in an all-female environment. Although the classes are what we'd consider a hybrid approach to reaching women, they offer the stores an excellent forum for feedback and an opportunity to learn firsthand what women want from their retail outlets and business organizations.

Also, *follow the dollars.* Tracking product spending by women and noting the departments with a strong spike in sales provides valuable information for companies. For example, Lowe's found that women are tackling more challenging projects, with more than 27 percent undertaking major renovations on their own, such as adding a sunroom or tearing down load-bearing walls. By tracking spending patterns, companies can get a clearer view of the scope of women's interests.

4. FOCUS ON YOUR PRODUCT'S CONTEXT. Being *information hungry and visually oriented* is important. The most difficult part of home improvement is visualizing the process. When a person can actually see how it's done, they feel empowered to undertake the project. While television and live seminars do the best job of meeting this need, home improvement stores are also tailoring their displays and services to be more visually informative. Craftsman Tools is targeting female buyers with detailed photo displays, and newer Ace retail locations feature in-store libraries packed with how-to information on household projects.

More shoppable environments are important also. Home improvement retailers have had to explore and respond to the different ways that women shop compared to men. Both Lowe's and Home Depot emphasize offering a more shoppable environment than that of the traditional hardware store. Lowe's spokeswoman Chris Ahearn says the company has been redesigning its stores since the late 1980s and early 1990s, and the company is continuing to evolve its design to appeal to women: "We really look at the way women shop because they are the decision-makers in the home," Ahearn says. "We want to make sure they are very comfortable in our stores so they can buy the items on their to-do list and also take the time to look around to get inspiration for their next project."[8] Ahearn says North Carolina–based Lowe's has made an effort to provide brighter lighting and wider aisles than its competitors in an effort to appeal to women shoppers. The stores also feature open and uncluttered spaces, clear signage and a home organization section. And, Ace Hardware has changed its signage and display lighting to better appeal to their women customers and to provide a more enhanced shopping experience.

5. UNDERSTAND AND DEFINE YOUR BRAND. Make it a *weekend destination and cool hobby.* Home improvement has morphed into a fun, satisfying and empowering weekend activity. In response, the industry is mixing education with entertainment, resulting in hit TV shows like *Trading Spaces*, interactive and social how-to seminars, and a slew of new books that feature attractive magazine-style layouts. A study conducted by Home Depot and Yankelovich Partners proves that home improvement is a cool hobby for women.[9] An amazing 37 percent said they would rather do home improvements than hit the malls (28 percent) or cook (25 percent). In fact, 54 percent of women versus 51 percent of men said they are currently undertaking some home improvement project.

A *showroom feel* is good. Women approach home improvement from the overall point of view of creating a home, not just fixing this or that. Showroom displays and room vignettes help women visualize the projects they'd like to do. For example, Home Depot expanded its design-related departments and gave their stores more of a showroom feel.

I remember going to the hardware store with my father when I was little, but my mom never joined us. It was dark and cluttered, and an unknown world for me. Now I go to one of the national chains on a regular basis and on my own, without my husband, to get inspiration for home repair and decorating projects. The place is light and well-organized, and the staff usually don't roll their eyes when I ask them dumb questions about copper fittings or lawn mowers.

—Claudia G., age 46, internet media specialist

More diversified and higher-end product offerings are helpful too. Home improvement stores are offering more designer lines, higher-end brands, and a larger selection of products that spark ideas for decorating. For example, to catch the attention of women shoppers, Lowe's has started carrying more designer lines, such as Laura Ashley paint and window coverings.

6. BE AUTHENTIC. By approaching women customers as the DIYers they are, and making their products, services and seminars relevant to women, home improvement retailers are reflecting a true commitment, not a phony ploy. The changes they've made in the past ten years reflect an honest and direct approach to their key customers. Women don't want to be ignored or spoken down to when they are standing in the aisles of their local retailer, and places like Ace Hardware, Lowe's and Home Depot have been enthusiastically embracing this new breed of home improvers.

In providing an exceptional shopping experience for customers, many stores in the hardware and home repair industry are learning how to develop long-term, one-on-one relationships with existing customers, as well as inspire newcomers. This industry has adopted an under-the-radar, transparent approach to marketing that is definitely reaching women more effectively.

Transparent Marketing Secrets

A transparent approach guides marketers to go beyond the obvious and truly tailor programs for the community they want to reach. Here are some secrets used by the best transparent marketers in the business:

1. SHOW HER "REAL" WOMEN AND RELATABLE SCENARIOS. For the last twenty years, in survey after survey, women have told advertisers that their advertising offers little for them to identify with. Women want brands they feel a connection with and which they can visualize themselves using. The most effective brands deliver a fun, relatable or thought-provoking "that's me" moment to spur her interest in the product or service.

It can be tempting for advertisers to depict women as one-dimensional creatures; and many current campaigns emphasize extremes, for example, representing a woman as either totally in control or completely frazzled. Related to this is portraying the same overused cast of stereotyped characters—the soccer mom, the superwoman executive or the minivan-carpooling mom.

But the reality is that women respond to authentic connections and are drawn to what is real rather than ideal. Marketers should strive to give their women customers an actual human being with whom to connect and from whom they can learn. They should also try to present some typical world diversity and introduce more interesting multidimensional personalities. Mary Lou Quinlan, CEO of Just Ask a Woman, a leading marketing consultant who specializes in women consumers, has worked with leading Fortune 500 companies to make their advertising more relevant to women.[10] She suggests adding dimension by playing against typecasting: "The serious executive can dance the merengue, the plain girl laughs wildly, the glamorous next-door neighbor is a cleaning maniac." Seeing more fully developed personalities would certainly catch the attention of potential consumers, and it would probably more accurately reflect the dichotomies of your typical customers' lives as well.

One of the reasons I love the Title 9 athletic wear catalog is that the women wearing the clothes look real. Then, you read the captions and realize that many of the models are also actually employees or friends of the company, instead of professional models. That's pretty cool.

—Robyn K., age 32, retail store owner and full-time mother of two

2. FOCUS ON CONNECTION AND TEAMWORK. No matter how you slice it, competition is simply not an underlying or driving force for most women. Clichéd or sexist as it may sound, women generally strive to get along and avoid conflict. They prefer teamwork because they know that finding a way for everyone to win most often produces the best results.

Collaborative interaction is important for women. Although prospering and fulfilling ambitions are strong motivators for both genders, for women it's rarely about getting ahead of the Joneses or about putting people down. Women, in general, don't respond to messages that reflect women one-upping men. Rather, focus on the things that typically hold great value for women. Present your product or service in relationship to the truest moments of a woman's daily life: for example, her close relationships or friendships, her children's accomplishments, her work, her achieving her *personal* best, her efforts to make the world a better place and her desire to occasionally get away from the stress of life.

3. CAPTURE HER IMAGINATION BY USING STORIES. A well-developed and well-told story can help her see how a product or service fits in her life. In that way, you will have given women the tools to create, imagine and envision how they will interact with your brand and reap its benefits. How will your brand help her get what she wants? How will it fit into her day? Forget your technical facts and figures or detailed explanations about how your product works. Tell the story of how your new-fangled product will make her life easier; and you can omit that it does so with rack and pinion anything or a gazillion bytes of RAM.

Consider the car commercials focused on speed, torque and precision curves or the computer ad driven by a bulleted list of RAM, memory and other techno-features. Where are the people? How does this product fit into her life? How will it make her life better?

Many of the ad campaigns for cell phones with built-in cameras, for example, are doing a great job of storytelling. Who'd have thought anyone would ever need or want a minicamera in their phone, or could find a regular use for it? But, ads succeed in telling a compelling by story showing a young man laughing about something he sees, then using his cell phone to take a picture and instantly send it off to a friend—a persuasive story of keeping friendship alive in real-time and sharing experiences in new ways.

4. MAKE IT MULTISENSORY. As Helen Fisher so well put it in her book, *The First Sex*, women tend to think in terms of "interrelated factors, not straight lines," while men have a "compartmentalized, incremental reasoning process."[11] Given what Fisher calls women's "web thinking," it makes sense to consider what a female consumer sees, hears, smells, feels and touches in relation to your brand. Women are taking it all in—much more so than men.

They are listening to the background music in your store; they are noticing the palette of your Web site; and they are getting a feeling of your brand by reading your site's copy or marketing materials. They are taking note of the music, words and feel of your ads, and they are getting a sense of touch from the materials you use to make your shop's doors and door handles. Your brand language needs to integrate and appeal to any of a woman's senses with which it comes into contact.

5. ADD THE LITTLE EXTRAS. The cost to a manufacturer for going the extra 10 percent is often negligible. There is no real cost to adding a hidden track to one of Norah Jones' CDs, but it can make a buyer feel as though they are getting something extra. Once people start talking about the cool "extra" you've presented to them, the buzz will begin and will inspire much loyalty. (See more below about creating customer evangelists.)

A fairly typical example is the way clothing retailers like The Gap use e-announcements to give regular customers a special code word to obtain an online discount. A recent example occurred when one of us (Andrea) received a free *Madonna & Missy* two-track CD in the package with The Gap cords she ordered. These extras can involve minimal expense, but much feel-good for the customers—as well as incentives for them to continue to read your e-mails and buy online.

6. TAP THE EMOTIONAL POWER OF MUSIC. For so many women, especially Gen Xers and Gen Yers, music provides the soundtrack of their lives. (Nothing like an old Jimmy Buffet song to make a few of us reminisce about the bliss of summer days on the beach.) Music can be an incredibly effective tool for marketers, particularly when developing brands that will appeal to the Gen Y market.

A study conducted by SUNY Stony Brook and Stanford University identified how women's brains process emotional imagery differently from men's brains. As it turns out, women do remember emotional events with greater clarity and detail (as we suspected), and all because they use a larger portion of their brain to process them. So tap into emotion with music and women may pay more attention to what your brand says.

7. CREATE CUSTOMER EVANGELISTS. Make your customers the center of your strategy, and they'll feel a sense of ownership and be inspired to lead the charge in your marketing efforts. As so well presented by Jackie Huba and Ben McConnell in their book, *Creating Customer Evangelists*, "when customers are truly thrilled about their experience with your product or service, they become outspoken 'evangelists' for your company."[12] And, customer evangelism is part and parcel of transparent marketing. According to Huba and McConnell, the six tenets of the concept are:

1. Continuously gather customer feedback.

2. Make it a point to share knowledge freely.

3. Build word-of-mouth networks.

4. Encourage community of customers to meet and share.

5. Devise specialized, smaller offerings to get customers initially interested.

6. Focus on making the world, or your industry, better.

8. FORM BRAND ALLIANCES. Since no brand can be everything for everybody, building partnerships is key to extending the reach of your transparent marketing. As brand expert Martin Lindstrom puts it, "The strategy ensures consumers are exposed to favored brands in new contexts, their product knowledge expands, and their brand use becomes more versatile."[13]

Starbucks is way ahead of that curve in developing synergistic alliances—with grocery stores, book chains and airlines, for example. As long as the alliances with your brand really do serve your customers, the synergies can only expand the effectiveness of your omnipresent transparent campaign.

Nice Try, but Not Quite Transparent

There are some brands that are clearly making an effort to connect with their female customers, but are still falling short of transparency. Their marketing teams may have skipped a few elements in their research or not fully examined their brand before churning out a women-focused ad. Following is a checklist of some key elements to keep you in touch with reality (and in authentic relationships with women) while you develop your brand's transparent campaign:

Avoid going overboard. Lisa Finn, editor of EPM Communications' *Marketing to Women* newsletter, observed that the Yoplait yogurt's "girlfriend series" ads could come across as artificial rather than charming.[14] She noted, ". . . [W]ho sits around trading increasingly unlikely comparisons for yogurt? There's something about putting a product so center-stage in a casual conversation that strikes a false note." If you tune into how your customers are really talking about your product, you won't create drama where it doesn't exist.

Avoid insincerity. It may seem fun and hip, but the "you go girl" tone can seem disingenuous these days when used for the wrong reasons. Focus on things that are important to women, not on trendy phrases or looks. Appealing to women's interest in healthier alternatives (like salads at Wendy's) or to their sense of humor (like the Subway sandwich commercials that include family laughs) will form a much more enduring connection.

Avoid sappiness. While it may be more realistic showing women in groups in ads, as opposed to standing around with their husbands, avoid the tendency to over-sentimentalize the situations. Done poorly, sappy ads can make everyone, female or male, roll their eyes—and that feeling may well stick with them when they come across your brand in the store aisle. Our advice: Get input from women in the street before you choose the final photos for your campaigns.

Avoid sexism. Your staff and your marketing team do not need to be all female, so don't make that mistake in your ads or promotions. First, having only women everywhere doesn't reflect the reality of the world or of your company and its consumers, and so it would come off as inauthentic in your marketing. Second, the fresh and creative thinking your brand needs to be relevant with women must be gender neutral. The final bonus is that the men on your marketing-to-women team and in the ranks of your customer service personnel will serve as the ever-important male-turnoff radar for any campaign you develop.

Avoid embellishments. Reaching women effectively is all about engaging in an honest and direct dialogue with them. It should be easy for women to get your point, without extras or exaggerations. If a product is purposely designed to improve a woman's health, for example, women shouldn't have to wonder whether it is a beauty product because the packaging emphasizes those features.

Avoid "noise." Be different and be first, and women will notice. There's no need to be the loudest in order to be heard in a transparent campaign. In fact, loudness—in color, design, interactivity and hit-you-over-the-head copy—can turn women off completely.

If we used the colloquial phrase "keep it real" to describe the one general guideline for transparently reaching women, we'd probably be accused of oversimplifying or being trite. Instead, we encourage you to revisit the idea of seeing your brand through a woman's perspective. How does she see you, hear your ads, absorb your television spots or take in your sponsorship of events?

Transparency Gives Women the Clearest Perspective

A transparent campaign will reflect your actual knowledge of your female customers, not your guesstimates or assumptions about women in general. The idea, for example, that all women respond favorably to the color purple would be a huge, mistaken assumption. Learning what features and benefits of your product, or which delivery methods and marketing strategies, will resonate most with women may at first not seem worth the additional research time. However, honing in on those details will indeed provide significant payoff in your long-term transparent efforts.

Since we know how a woman's particular generation, her roles, life stages and cultural influencers all filter her buying mind, it makes sense to keep your marketing efforts authentic and transparent. Women have enough to sift through on a daily basis, so they'll be that much more receptive to your brand if it somehow works its way into their lives without fanfare.

True transparency means your brand shouldn't have to make an effort to appear authentic; rather it should effortlessly be doing what it takes to genuinely connect with women. Serving women in this way requires that your brand stay in sync with the way women think and live, presenting them with solutions and supplying them with products and services—where and when they need them. Now that's a custom-tailored approach.

CHAPTER 4

inside a woman's mind
the scientific underpinnings

THE BUYING MINDS of women are sophisticated and powerful tools. In most cases, women engage in an involved decision-making process, seldom just a simple "see it and buy it." They may come across the product once or twice, think about it, research it online, ask their friends and restart the process several times, factoring in the new input before ever pulling out their checkbooks.

We can practically guarantee that studying up, even a little bit, on what goes on in her buying mind will help your company identify the characteristics that will lead her interest and loyalty your way. It will also help you develop a killer transparent marketing approach.

The Science of a Woman's Perspective

Self-help authors haven't just fabricated the idea to sell books: Men and women *do* think differently. Studies have shown that there are biological, neurological and behavioral variations between the male and female brains. And, of course, these gender-specific brain differences have a profound effect on the way information is absorbed, processed and retained.

So, while traditional marketing strategies were likely designed to spark the imaginations of men, a bit more knowledge of how a woman's mind works is critical for marketers in the twenty-first century. Below we've included snapshots of those differences in the way male and female brains process information that seemed most applicable to what goes on in a woman's buying mind.[1]

1. A WOMAN'S BRAIN SYNERGY. We first summarize the basics for understanding women's brains and their brain synergy, before we translate that for the marketing realm. (A good reference has been Brainplace.com.[2])

First, though men may have more brain cells than women do, women have more dendritic (fiber) connections between brain cells. This may explain why women tap so many senses and see a bigger picture when making a buying decision (or any other decision, for that matter). From what they see (for example, packaging), to what they hear (background music in a store or the jingle in an ad) and how they feel (an emotional connection to an advertising message), their brain cells are connecting and sharing information at all levels.

A female brain has larger connecting tissue, or corpus collusum, which means women can transfer data between the right and left hemispheres faster. If there's more room in which those decision-making brainwaves can mix and mingle, perhaps that's what makes it easier for women to compile diverse input and come to a decision. Men do tend to have larger brains and to be more left brained (linear), while women have greater access to both sides (more holistic thinkers) of their usually smaller-sized brains.

Furthermore, current research has demonstrated that females, on average, have a larger deep limbic system than males, which means that they are more in touch with their feelings, and so are generally better able than men to express them. It follows, then, that women are also tapped into emotionally charged images. A recent study conducted by psychologists at the State University of New York and Stanford University found that, though emotion-evoking photographs were more likely than emotionally flat images to stick in the brains of both men and women, women were able to remember more of the emotional images over time than could men.[3] In addition to these findings indicating women use more of their brains to process emotional images, women have also been found to have an increased ability to bond with and be connected to others—which equip them generally to be the best caretakers of children.

So, it's a fact. A woman's brain functions differently than a man's. This is *not* a debate about which gender's brain is better, per se, because each is simply different in form and function. Being aware of these differences gives us a sound basis from which to launch our consideration of female-focused marketing approaches. Three of the applications we can quickly connect to these brain facts are:

MARKETING TO A WOMAN'S BRAIN SYNERGY

It all matters. Surveys show that most women perceive a brand's products and marketing more holistically than men do, which may reflect the quick connection between women's left and right brain lobes. How a company treats its employees, what it espouses environmentally, how it invests or whether its corporate causes are socially responsible may all influence a woman's decision to make a purchase. A woman's wide-angle perspective can simultaneously take in products and politics, people and businesses, in order to give her brain the complete picture she prefers before making a final, wise buying decision.

Inconsistencies are noticed. Because women are so aware of and interested in all aspects of doing business with your company, they will be quick to spot inconsistent messages. If your company says one thing but does another, take heed. When an inconsistency is exposed, you risk more than losing a customer; you risk sparking a disenchanted woman's desire to share her negative perspective with her personal network of friends and family.

Human connections are key. No matter what the product or service, a brand should recognize that women are not living in their own little "me, me, me" vacuum. Rather, they are almost always thinking of their family, friends and neighbors. If your brand can help a woman help her family or help her stay connected with friends— for example, by easing the morning breakfast rush with your cereal, or providing an easy way to tell a friend about your Web site— you've tapped into her human connections.

2. A WOMAN'S OBSERVATIONAL SKILLS. Women can take in information on many levels, and typically absorb a much greater amount of it from their environments than do men. As part of their more holistic life perspective, women are continually integrating the many facets of their daily lives. Whether they notice an inconsistency between your product presentation and the actual product, or the seemingly trivial positioning of objects in a room, women's brains are more likely to grab and process such input. And, if there is an emotional element involved, their brains are even more likely to remember and ruminate about it in their decision-making phase.

Once you realize that women notice more of what goes on around them and so will likely also notice what a brand is representing outside of its product offerings, you have no excuse to ignore those elements. Your female customer is ultraobservant, so give her some incredible detail to absorb and digest. The more positively she perceives your brand's profile, the better.

MARKETING TO A WOMAN'S OBSERVATIONAL SKILLS

Be in her peripheral vision. Identify and review any possible place where your brand or logo might surface or linger in a woman's daily life. Seemingly secondary elements like the music playing in your store, or the training of your sales staff, or the complementary products you offer at the point of purchase could all be considered peripheral-vision brand extensions as well. You may want to ask yourself: Are the peripheral messages of my brand consistent with its overall marketing message? Or, does the brand pop up in places that don't make sense, and thus confuse my consumers? Title 9 Sports, a women's athletic clothing catalog, for example, only sponsors projects and events that help young women get more active. This helps them from showing up in incongruent places like a financial seminar or a county fair.

It's weird, but when I'm in a Starbucks, I expect pleasant background music, friendly baristas, interesting gift ideas and clean restrooms. If the music was ever just blaring Britney Spears, I swear I'd feel dizzy. It just wouldn't fit.

—Jami Y., age 30, e-learning specialist

Integrate marketing and media channels. Studies show that if your Web store doesn't serve up a customer experience consistent with that of your retail store, it affects your entire brand's reputation and, in some cases, may cost you a faithful customer. As women head online in full shopping force, brands that may have rested on their off-line brick-and-mortar laurels will need to fine-tune their Web site's customer experience to deliver to those high expectations.

3. A WOMAN'S SENSE OF DISCOVERY. Whether the behavior is scientifically based or not, it's probably safe to say there is truth to the observation that women are more likely to ask for driving directions than men.[4] What is at the root of that? When women explore, they want to know how to reach their destination in advance, so they can better relax and enjoy the trip. For men, perhaps getting to a destination efficiently may not be as important as their belief that they can find it themselves (eventually), and so they don't fret the extra time spent taking wrong turns.

The same is true for women in the consumer realm: They would rather do front-end research and then go straight to the one product that meets their needs, than try five different products over the course of a few months. In their minds, there is no use in wasting time and money not being completely satisfied. For women, the pre-purchase process is much more important than it is for men; because that's when women ask all their questions and eliminate potential mistakes and time wasters.

A woman's discovery process also gives her a way to reach out to people as she seeks purchasing advice—tuning in, yet again, to her tendency to seek human connections. In questioning others, women are ever the multitaskers, building new relationships while locating the best product in the least amount of time.

MARKETING TO A WOMAN'S SENSE OF DISCOVERY

Support her inquisitive nature. When they are in a comfortable sales environment, women tend to ask more questions; so you may want to reevaluate whether your store's lighting and decor are too industrial or uncomfortable and thus off-putting to women. Furthermore, as we found through our own observation of classroom situations, seminars and workshops, women tend to participate more and share more information about a new topic when the group is all female. (Interestingly, it doesn't seem to matter as much whether the instructor is male or female.) When the audience is mixed, women seem to revert to limiting their participation, not asking questions or sharing their experiences and stories.

Provide all of the information. Product benefits and features that may seem pretty basic in your eyes might be especially important to women, so it's worth emphasizing those. If you sell computers, for example, even though your free technical phone support may only meet the industry standard, that offering will be just as important to women as the product's processing speed and storage capacity, if not more so.

Plug into her ongoing education. Most women consumers approach new product purchasing decisions with the desire to educate themselves for future reference, which can be very empowering. So, an educational approach and tone may strengthen the marketing of your brand. Use information-based formats, not salesy spiels, for brochures, seminars, e-mail newsletters and Web sites. Don't rush women through the sales process, but allow time for questions and information at all customer touch points. Online, don't require her to fill in long sign-up forms as gateways to further information; and avoid dumping product searches straight into the checkout area.

4. A WOMAN'S SENSE OF VALUES. Women think inclusively more than exclusively. They see life, on the whole, through a wide-angle rather than a telephoto lens. It is important to women as consumers to know there are others out there like themselves who are pleased with your product. Their inclusive values may also mean that, where appropriate, they'd prefer to buy brands that donate a percentage of sales or profits to a respected charity. This is quite different from the competitive or hierarchical motivators (like "bigger" or "newest") that may spur men to purchase.

Because a woman's values can be so integral to her purchasing decisions, connecting with her on this level may be all the more important. Whether a woman is a traditionally conservative shopper or someone whose environmental concerns are her greatest priority, here are two ways to ensure your marketing efforts will speak to her values:

MARKETING TO A WOMAN'S SENSE OF VALUES

Select messages, images and stories with care. Select copy, themes and graphics that authentically reflect the values of your female customers. For example, a woman's need to get more financially savvy should be presented positively, not as a reason for anxiety, in the marketing materials or Web site of a financial planning company. Where guilt can cause indecision, knowing that taking control of your finances sets you up for a richer, more empowered life will more likely inspire action.

Connect women to one another around your brand. Whenever possible, incorporate the voices, feedback and images of women who are your existing customers. Nothing rings truer to new customers or Web site visitors, or builds a connection more quickly, than the personal testimony or smiling face of another happy customer. Where possible and appropriate, photographs of actual customers along with their testimonials can bring positive words to life.

Make improving a woman's life your brand's context. While they don't often come right out and ask it (at least most of us don't), the overarching question for many women consumers is: How will this product or service make my life better? So, redevelop, rename or repackage your existing stellar products and services to resonate with this priority. Two examples include:

- A few years back Dodge Caravan designed a minivan with a built-in television and DVD accessory, which put their product in the context of blissfully quiet road trips. Their ad campaign showcased the vehicle during a bicker-free trip as kids wearing headphones giggled at the TV screen.

▫ Mary Kay Cosmetics has guided thousands of women into entrepreneurship by offering them an opportunity to "Be in business for yourself . . . but not by yourself." They have effectively shifted the concept of owning a business away from the fear of isolation and lack of support and into a new context of being part of a large supportive community. That's delivering the same "package," but with a reworked marketing approach that resonates with women's values.

Time has become today's currency, so many women will see huge value in paying slightly more for products and services that give them more time in their day. Make saving time for your customers a high priority if you want to become a brand that helps ease a woman's daily task-mastering duties. To give her that impression, you might:

SIMPLIFY A WOMAN'S LIFE BY SAVING HER TIME

Test every step of the sales process with a stopwatch. Too-busy customer-service phones, inadequate online services, lengthy forms and hard-to-understand copy are all things that require your scrutiny and tweaking when your goal is to serve women better.

Offer flexible business hours. Consider whether your business would benefit from extending its after-work hours, staying open on weekends or offering additional customer service phone hours. Veterinarians have benefited from maintaining less traditional office hours, as women often take care of most of their household pets' medical care needs.

Promote the time-saving aspects of your product or service. Women may need a reminder to see your product in a time-saving light, so come up with the best ways to promote those benefits. Enterprise Rent-A-Car, for example, is luring busy travelers by picking up people at their homes. Even if they aren't regular travelers, women who see Enterprise ads will store that information for later use or refer-ence. Case in point, even though one of us (Lisa) has never used it, she has told many people about the service.

Fine-tune your Web site's download and navigation times. Whether your customers have broadband access or are still on dial-up, it is unacceptable for your site to have lengthy download times or to require too many clicks to find something (the industry standard is no more than three clicks to find the answer or product, and no more than eight seconds for downloads). Otherwise, most customers, no matter their gender, will leave your site to shop elsewhere.

Evaluate the best use of each customer touch point. Keep track of how much your customers use the various channels of interaction with your brand. From your Web site and telephone customer service to your retail outlets or direct mail, you've got to use a woman's time wisely, so integrate your channels accordingly. For example, a com-puter manufacturer discovered that the Web was great for provid-ing product information, but challenging for tech support and returns. In response, they built retail stores complete with tech cen-ters, so repairs and returns could be dropped off. For service-oriented businesses in particular, stellar online service backed up by phone service, and possible in-person meetings, are ideal.

5. A WOMAN'S COMMUNICATION STYLE. It may be no sur-prise that women have a distinct advantage in terms of language skills. For men, language resides most often in just the dominant hemisphere (usually the left), but a larger number of women seem to be able to use both sides of their brains for language.[5]

To that end, sociolinguist Deborah Tannen has observed that men are more often inclined to jockey for status in a conversation, while women are more often inclined to negotiate connections.[6] For women, communicating is about building bonds and forging relationships based on mutual values and interests.

Both men and women joke about how much women seem to like to talk, whether it's about relationships or this season's shoe styles. But, communication is important to women, and their propensity to be involved in interaction is a real plus for marketers. Following are some good ways to reflect your awareness of women's communication styles in your marketing efforts:

MARKETING TO A WOMAN'S COMMUNICATION STYLE

Avoid over-automation, at all costs. Women tend to be the hold-outs in this high-tech era of ours. Whether through phone, e-mail or online chat, many women still like to feel the presence of a human being or some sort of authentic personal connection on the other end of any communication during the buying process. This means you should, for example, consider humanizing your marketing efforts by including value-based content (like testimonials and success stories), or by posting your 800 number prominently to show your brand's accessibility to a woman's questions or concerns.

Update your relationship-building opportunities. Match the way women connect outside your industry with the ways you try to reach them. For example, if you truly want to reach women in a woman's way, mass-marketed seminars might evolve into learning environments on the human scale of book clubs, and focus groups could become conversational gatherings in relaxed locations like day spas.

After all, book clubs and spas are today much more common in a woman's life than large conferences or classroom seminars. Furthermore, as society reflects a growing interest in coaching for self-growth, it makes sense to train your sales people to develop more relationship-based, one-on-one experiences with your customers (especially women).

Facilitate story sharing. Additional education and training to reach women can come from your existing customers. So, you might consider providing or hosting a forum through which your women customers can share their stories with one another. Because so few companies are tapping into this aspect of a woman's communication style, women will remember the brand that helped them find a solution-oriented community, and they will remain loyal and very likely spread the word about it to their friends.

For example, Christiane Northrup, M.D., author of *The Wisdom of Menopause*, did just that when she established her own hugely successful clinic as a place for women to share their stories, receive medical guidance and discover more health-enhancing ways to live their lives.[7] In addition to serving the overall needs of her patients, Dr. Northrup listened to hundreds of women talk about the issues of menopause, catapulting her to the forefront of the menopause-care community. She is now a leading expert on menopause and her work serves as a key resource for many women.

The Art of How She Buys

Now that we've touched on the science of a woman's brain, and how to apply some of those insights to marketing more effectively, let's take a closer look at the art of her buying behavior. For a woman, the process of buying is much more complicated than simply thinking up a need and rushing to the store with credit card in hand. We've broken the art into four key characteristics that define what goes into women's typical buying processes. We've also added a few comments from women to demonstrate each characteristic.

1. WOMEN DEVELOP AND USE SMART SHOPPING SKILLS.

First of all, good old hands-on experience and simple observation combine to make women smart shoppers right from the start. Most women have grown up watching their mothers manage households, so shopping efficiently comes almost second nature to them.

Whether selecting a stock or finding a pediatrician, the majority of women go through a buying process that involves, in no particular order: consulting friends, comparison shopping, checking several reference resources and getting validation from trusted experts or word-of-mouth sources (including their family).

To sales people or her own family, a woman's prepurchase mulling over big-ticket items, or emotionally significant or first-time purchases, can seem overly thorough (and feel like it takes forever). However, once she completes her due diligence and identifies the best product or service to purchase, a woman will often stay brand loyal longer. She put a lot of upfront effort into learning the industry and making comparisons and, unless proven otherwise, will hold onto her trust in that decision.

I am willing to spend more time doing research before I make a new purchase, because I know from experience that it will cost me time, energy and money to correct a mistake. My goal is not to make just a good choice, but to make the best choice for me.

—Kim O., age 29, accountant

HOW TO SUPPORT WOMEN'S SMART SHOPPING SKILLS

Create a sales culture that is committed to helping women determine the best choice, not to closing the quickest sale.

Equip, encourage and empower your sales and customer-service staff to go the extra mile and take the added time for customers and prospects. Nordstrom is famous for empowering their sales people to make the exchange process simple, easy and even pleasant. At a Nordstrom store, you can just relax and conduct your business, knowing that you'll never have to concoct an elaborate reason for exchanging goods.

Where possible, companies should enable the same customer service representative to work with a customer until their needs are resolved (whether that takes thirty minutes or thirty days). Companies with large-scale customer support would certainly find such personal attention too costly, so a code number that follows customer service inquiries throughout the system would be a sufficient compromise. Whatever you do, give your staff the leeway to access any customer's record, anytime, to save the customer from having to retell her entire tale of frustration every time she calls for a status report.

2. WOMEN ARE CONSTITUENT-DRIVEN DECISION MAKERS. Women set their priorities according to the needs of the people most dear to them, their "constituents." No matter what the topic, a woman's perspective will lead her to include in her point of view her spouse, significant other, children, grandchildren, aging parents, employees, friends and, yes, even her pets. So, rather than being "all about me," the purchases made or directly influenced by a female consumer are more often than not for or about her loved ones.

Women typically have the responsibility for the majority of household purchasing decisions, running the gamut from real estate and financial services to major household goods and automobiles. As we already know, women make the majority of consumer purchases and sign the most personal checks and credit and debit card slips as well. That noted, patronizing women or treating them as though they were industry-ignorant during any contact in a purchasing process, from information gathering to possible returns, would likely end a customer relationship before it even started.

More traditionally male-dominated industries, like the marine industry for example, might have to try a little harder to overcome treating women or new-to-industry consumers in a condescending manner. In fact, when we talked with a boat manufacturer's female marketing director recently, she told us that she still occasionally witnessed salesmen (yes, still mostly men) at boat shows making eye contact only with the husband or boyfriend, and at times actually giving the woman *buyer* the cold shoulder.

Can you make sure you are honoring your female customers as the legitimate purchase decision-makers they are?

HOW TO SUPPORT HER CONSTITUENCY CONCERNS AND DECISIONS

Identify and assist the ways in which women support family members (husband, kids, aging parents) with purchases. For example, women often play the doctor role in their families and are involved in the majority of all health-care decisions, including the purchase of over-the-counter drugs or remedies. So, help them keep track of their many family prescriptions; and, gather information (where appropriate and with permission) that will help you offer discounts for the items or brands they frequently purchase.

My radar is always on, so I'm continuously picking up information that will solve a future problem for my dad or someone else in my family. I tend to be the one who does all the shopping legwork to identify and buy the product we need.

—Kris H., age 38, dental assistant

Position your services and offers based on how they will benefit the others in her life as well as her. A department store's one-stop shopping that serves entire families is one standard example of this concept. A few more examples include: Jiffy Lube shops that now have a child's play area in their waiting rooms; and financial planners who now offer information on retirement for women as well as information to help them guide their aging parents with post-retirement financial decisions.

Educate your staff (all of them) to serve women well, right from the start. Make sure they know your customer demographics and realize the value and buying power of women. The beginning, or investigative, stage of a woman's purchasing process presents an important opportunity to foster brand loyalty and trust. Women are more inclined to purchase from the brands that equip them with relevant information and treat them right long before money changes hands. Body language and inclusiveness speak volumes. Always have your staff make eye contact with women customers, or create a similar honest and direct presence online. Furthermore, be sure to structure inclusive conversations that respect her opinions and concerns, and provide an environment that encourages deeper questions about your product or service.

3. WOMEN SEEK ONGOING RELATIONSHIPS AND INSIDER INFORMATION.

When a woman is ready to try a new product or service, her first research step is to turn to someone who already owns and uses it. The insider is that person who provides credible, hard-to-find information on an unfamiliar product or industry, and who a woman can perceive as unbiased and trustworthy. In most cases, the perfect insider may well be a friend who is also a fellow consumer of that product, but there are some exceptional sales people and a few specific personalities who can earn this coveted insider role as well (for example, Oprah Winfrey on her book and product recommendations). And, in the cyber world, the e-mails on NYC and LA Daily Candy (www.daily-candy.com), with all their references to little-known and out-of-the-way shops and restaurants, can certainly feel like the inside scoop from a friend.

HOW TO SUPPORT HER GATHERING OF INSIDER INFORMATION

Recognize, respect and utilize the power of a woman's personal network by providing pass-along devices (online and print) and by seeking referrals. Give women a quick and easy way to share their newfound knowledge with others. For example, include "Send to a friend" and "Printer version" features on relevant e-mail messages or Web pages.

Maintain some level of interaction (live or via e-mail) through all phases of the marketing, sales and customer-service cycle.

Understand and honor the fact that some purchasing decisions may take longer to make because of the time a woman may need to solicit the opinions of others. No need to rush when you are trying to earn a woman's trust.

I always ask the advice of people who I already know own the product. It's the fastest way to zero in on what few brands I should consider. Since they have nothing to gain from telling me about their experiences, I trust what they have to say.

—Darcy P., age 23, office manager

If women feel they've forged a connection with your company during the information-gathering and pre-sale process, they will expect that same sort of relationship to continue into the post-purchase, product-support phase. (Interestingly, according to retail anthropologist Paco Underhill, men often prefer to gather information from product displays and brochures, rather than seek out the personal touch in their buying process that is so important to women.)[8]

WAYS TO FORGE AN ONGOING RELATIONSHIP

Provide women with both the information and the time to discuss, assimilate and understand it.

Provide top-quality, well-trained personnel for customer-service roles via phone, e-mail or online chat.

Make sure that e-mails and Web pages provide and facilitate the use of a toll-free phone number and personalized e-mail addresses, rather than just "support@yourcompany.com."

Develop an expert personality, or "virtual human," who answers your Q&A—equipped with a personalized e-mail address and a team of people to draft responses. We can both attest that we'd rather pose questions directly to "Stan Johnson" at the home electronics retailer, for example, than to some anonymous "questions@homeelectronics retailer.com." Whether Stan really exists or is some team member who actually answers our e-mail isn't the issue: It feels more human and personalized to send questions to an actual name.

Rename and repackage your expert consultation and customer services to make them less intimidating and more accessible to novices. For example, free "financial coaching appointments" sounds more comfortable to a person in the investigative stage than does a "sales appointment" with a broker.

4. WOMEN COMPARISON SHOP. Just as women put their feelers out via their human networks, they will also gather data through their own reading and research. Especially when contemplating major purchases, women tend to spend time to educate themselves on the features, benefits, price range and reliability of the available brands. In addition to using traditional information resources, like magazine articles, television programs and buying guides, an increasing number of women now look to the Internet for further help, including the peer and expert recommendations available on sites like Epinions.com.

Starbucks built on peer recommendations and insider scoop by developing and selling "Artist's Choice" CDs, featuring compilations of songs that inspired popular artists like Sheryl Crow. It makes sense that people who enjoy Sheryl Crow's music might also like the music she recommends.

I usually investigate on my own to see how different products rate against each other, and the Internet has made that process a lot easier. In a few cases, I buy a book written on the topic and see what the author recommends.

—Annie L., age 63, retired teacher

It may seem counterintuitive, but a quality brand shouldn't fear comparison-shopping by its customers. Rather, such a brand should wholeheartedly encourage and support that process. After all, when a woman delves deep to find out more about an industry, she should decide that your product or service ranks right up there at the top!

HOW TO SUPPORT HER COMPARISON SHOPPING

Listen to women carefully in advance of developing your materials, and provide the specific education, programs and industry standards that will allow them greater confidence in making decisions related to your product or service.

Provide a comparison matrix of your product's features against those of its competitors. It's worth the risk. Even if a woman ends up buying one of the other brands this time, she will return to your site to do her research, realizing that your company is helping her the most with her decisions.

Include those things that might be considered insider information or expert opinion in your marketing materials (on- or off-line), such as consumer testimonials, expert reviews, awards and seals of approval.

Offer handouts and e-mail courses and advice on what to look for (and avoid) when making a purchase of this general type of product or service. Also, provide a resource list and recommend books and Web sites or online content (with links) to facilitate a woman's comparison shopping.

Her Buying Mind Is Just the Beginning

Once you learn more about a woman's buying mind, you will most certainly notice opportunities for your brand to serve her complex decision-making process. It isn't just about getting your product onto the shelf to sit silently in front of your potential customers while you hope they decide to buy it (based perhaps on its great package design or its placement on the shelf?). Rather, you can proactively help women see that they definitely need your time-saving widget, by going deeper than traditional marketing in reflecting the truths of their daily lives in your brand.

And, remember, how you serve her now should also convince her that she'll need your brand in the future. You don't go to all this length learning about your female customers to simply sell a product to her once.

A woman's buying mind is always turned on, locating products for herself as well as for her family and for any of her other constituents. Furthermore, she's usually seeking a bit of "value-add" beyond the purchase. By providing women with extra education, or helping them gain more confidence in making purchases in a new industry, the service component of your brand will be significantly enhanced in their minds.

A woman's buying mind is adept at seeing through the surface of marketing copy and zeroing in on the deeper value your brand can bring to her life.

So, work to develop your brand and its marketing approach to fit perfectly within the behavior of a woman's buying mind and the structure of her involved decision-making process. With time, you'll build up enough information about, and experience with, your savvy female customers that "the mystery of a woman's buying mind" will be eternal no more.

CHAPTER 5

shaping the generations
baby boomers (and matures) to gen yers

THERE ARE SO many ways to segment the women's market that it can be hard to know where to begin. But, if we start by examining the different experiences and life-shaping events of women born in different generations, we'll jump-start the process of identifying what is shaping the collective perspective of your women's market.

Tapping into the shared experiences and memories of such large groups can point to what drives these consumers' basic needs and wants. By taking the time to understand a generation of women in this way, and learning just what makes each age range unique, your marketing efforts will better reflect women's priorities. Your female customers will appreciate that your brand knows them, and they will be thankful that the products you are marketing to them are the ones they truly need.

The commonalities of people born within a certain generation, and the social and economic conditions they experienced together, can provide great insight about consumer behavior. Once you've read this chapter, we think you'll agree that the generational elements that shape consumers' viewpoints form a baseline for developing marketing strategies that will reach them.

The Generations[1]

Generation	Born	Age in 2003	Estimated Population	Estimated Women Population
Y	1980–1997	6–23	74.2 million	36.2 million
X	1965–1979	24–38	62.1 million	30.8 million
Baby Boomer	1945–1964	39–58	80.2 million	40.8 million
Mature	Before 1945	59+	50.7 million	28.7 million

While the generational insights covered in this chapter are true for large groups of women within each segment, we do not propose that these profiles fit all women within the given generation described. And, of course, plenty of men were also shaped in similar ways by their generational commonalities.

Generation Y Women

Look out. Having grown up with the personal computer and the Internet, Generation Y women are leading the charge in the twenty-first century. These young women in general also enjoy education and now outnumber men on college campuses and in graduate schools. Raised under the prosperity of Boomer parents whom they appreciate as role models, Gen Yers continue to expect things to go their way, and they'll stride right through any obstacles that may lie in their path.

The savvy buying minds of this segment have long since become the focus for retailers and moviemakers. The Internet, as familiar to Gen Y as TV was to their parents, is a critical channel through which to market goods, movies, music and services to them.

GENERATION Y'S BUYING FILTERS

The women of Generation Y will likely keep us all on our toes. As marketers we have to learn to speak to the unique experiences of their formative years (especially involving the Internet) and to resonate with their feelings of optimism and entitlement. In general, they are the most advertised-to generation in history and will likely expect even more from the brands that serve them than do the preceding generations. We have to be up to the challenges. Generation Y women are approximately 36.2 million strong, and they are destined to be a major market force and marketing focus for years to come.

The characteristics that may be influencing a Gen Y woman's view of your brand include:

Optimistic. Though they experienced the dot-com bust and 9/11, the wealth of their collective life perspective leads the members of Gen Y to view things with an overall sense of optimism and security.

Technology savvy. This digital generation has never known life without computers. And now, with cell phones, pagers and instant messaging all part of their daily lives, technology skills come naturally and new innovation is welcomed and expected. All of their interactions with technology have accustomed them to expect instant gratification. Girls ages 12 to 15 are among the fastest growing groups on the Internet.[2] And, nearly 70 percent of all twelve- to nineteen-year-olds go online each week.[3]

Doers. This generation prefers to learn by construction and discovery rather than instruction. They are active initiators and doers, rather than passive observers or absorbers.

Entitled. Thanks to their cocoon-like upbringings, this generation of young women will often expect results at lightning-quick speed—including their own fame and fortune.

Multicultural. From the first day of nursery school, these women have lived in a true melting pot of skin colors and cultural differences. They are racially diverse and familiar with multiculturalism. According to a recent Gallup survey of youth, this generation is the least prejudiced about race and the most dissatisfied with race relations.[4]

Individualistic. Their independence and self-reliance lead these women to look for products that suit their personal tastes and preferences: So, customization is key. They will look for ways to further personalize purchases even after they buy them. Jones Soda, for example, offers their customers their own five minutes of fame via its Web site, inviting loyal fans to send in a photograph of themselves for possible use on a Jones Soda label. So far more than sixty thousand labels are ready for production, and even though the odds are low—only forty are picked annually—the lure for Gen Yers is irresistible. If they don't get picked, Jones Soda lovers can also pay to have their picture on a customized twelve pack of bottles.

Education focused. Influenced by Baby Boom parents who valued education, and entering a workplace that demands it, most Gen Yers recognize that the key to their success lies in advanced learning. These women are continuing the trend of outnumbering men on college campuses (since 1979) and in graduate schools (since 1984).[5]

Socially conscious. Responding to messages from schools and churches that they can make a difference, Gen Yers are exhibiting a refreshing altruism that embraces the environment, poverty and community problems. According to Neil Howe and William Strauss, authors of *Millennials Rising: The Next Great Generation,*

"Surveys show that five out of six Gen Yers believe their generation has the greatest duty to improve the environment."[6]

Confused and stressed. Under all their optimism lies a healthy dose of confusion and stress. This period in life is, in fact, a whirlwind of new responsibilities and freedoms for Gen Yers that can make them feel helpless, indecisive and panicked. So prevalent is the feeling among Gen Yers that the term "quarterlife crisis" has been coined to describe it.[7]

Independent, yet collaborative. Gen Yers want to do things their own way, while still working enthusiastically in teams. They believe in their skills and are not shy about taking risks. Many Gen Yers are confident beyond their years and have taught their elders about technology.

Entrepreneurial. Until Gen Y, Gen X had been touted as the most entrepreneurial generation in American history. Encouraged by their predecessors, and often financed by their Baby Boomer parents, Gen Yers are starting their own businesses in record numbers. According to the Kansas City–based Kauffman Center for Entrepreneurial Leadership, in 2000 "more than 65 percent of fourteen- to nineteen-year-olds [were] interested in starting a business compared with about half of the general public."[8]

REFLECTING GEN Y WOMEN IN YOUR BRAND

The women of Gen Y are style-conscious and tech-savvy, so they appreciate flash and dazzle much more than their parents do. They expect things to come at them rapidly and loudly (figuratively and literally), and they also enjoy parodies of "way back when" in the 1980s, like the Old Navy retro television ads of the early 2000s.

Unless you have a few Gen Yers on your marketing team, you'll really need to pay attention in order to develop messages that authentically resonate with, and reflect the values of, this generation of women.

Giving Gen Y Women the Best Perspective of Your Brand

▫ Traditional mass media broadcasts of prepackaged content will be less likely to meet the steep expectations of Gen Y.

▫ Customized and highly personalized offerings will be in demand from this Internet generation.

▫ Self-discovery is a passion and a goal unto itself for Gen Y women. Quizzes and other forms of personal learning, packaged as entertainment, are a huge hit with them.

▫ Instead of explaining things to this generation, provide ways for them to actively discover what they want to know about your product or service via your Web site.

▫ By encouraging online sharing and comparing of information, you can incorporate the social aspects of shopping as much as possible into the online realm. For example, you might provide a tool to e-mail a photo of a shirt to a friend with the message, "I really liked this shirt, what do you think of it?"

▫ They are skeptical and sophisticated. Remember that these women have been targeted by countless marketing messages in their short lifetimes, so they are alert to advertising tricks—like unconvincing contests or incentives, or Internet pop-ups that mislead or reroute anyone who responds.

▫ They expect to find your brand represented across multiple media channels, with seamless integration between your online and off-line business units.

▫ Product placements in television shows and movies and sponsorships of concerts are hugely influential brand endorsements for this generation.

▫ Present these women with flash, dazzle and entertainment, but do it without slowing them down. They are tech-savvy, so they know it can be done.

▫ They fully expect offers of free stuff through contests and promotions.

▫ Target specific interests and provide a compelling offer in any e-mail copy delivered to Gen Y women. From their perspective, mass marketed copy is simply spam.

▫ Use peer word-of-mouth and viral marketing to reach these women. This generation's younger members, in particular, have been known to build powerful grassroots support for individual entertainers, recordings and films.

▫ Provide ways for Gen Y women to learn and then quickly personalize their experience with your product, service or brand. Personalization can come in the unique way they use your digital camera on their rafting trip in Colorado, for example; or in the way they creatively rework your product to make it more expressive of their own style—such as embroidering or painting their jeans.

Overall, Gen Y women are savvy and aware. As members of today's key emerging consumer group, they are an incredibly important segment of the women's market. A brand that works for these women, and around which they develop a sense of ownership, will reflect these women's own philosophies and voices. And because this is a generation of upgraders—of cell phones, cars and fashion—forging a lasting connection with them holds long-term importance for your brand.

While confusing and elusive to many marketers, Gen Y women represent an economic powerhouse that will grow only stronger as they enter the workforce en masse. As marketers, we should appreciate the ways they are different from their older siblings and parents, and treat them like the savvy consumers they are.

GEN Y INDUSTRY STUDY: MOBILE PHONE MANIA

With more than 50 percent of fifteen- to twenty-four-year-old Americans owners of mobile phones, it is no surprise that Generation Y outpaces all U.S. mobile users in minutes used, number of calls placed, messages sent and wireless data accessed. High ownership and usage statistics point to a strong connection between female Gen Yers, in particular, and their mobile phones. So these wireless communications devices represent much-valued freedom for these women.

Cell phones can give Gen Yers a sense of independence even while they are still bunking at home, living in dorms or sharing apartments. The text-messaging, Internet-accessing and picture-snapping capabilities of mobile phones also empower these women to create communities of friends on their own terms.

For example, young women can maintain constant contact with one another via text messaging, regardless of time or place. They can manage their social lives on-the-go, as they move from classroom to extracurricular activities, from mall to party, finally returning home. Given the way Gen Y has wholeheartedly embraced the cell phone, these young women will likely continue to eagerly adopt new data services as they are developed.

Boost Mobile LLC (a unit of Nextel Communications, Inc.), headquartered in Irvine, California, is a good example of how to tap into the technology lovefest of this younger generation. This lifestyle-based telecommunications business unit was expressly set up by Nextel to focus solely on developing and distributing communications products for the youth market, such as a pay-as-you-go wireless phone service with a two-way walkie-talkie; pay-as-you-go airtime cards and a wide range of accessories; Java games for wireless phones; downloadable ring-tones; and other cutting-edge mobile services. Boost Mobile's marketing efforts center on youth activities like action sports, music, fashion and entertainment, right down to the surf- and skateboarding action images on their mainly black-and-silver Web site.

Boost Mobile's further marketing efforts involve a partnership to create a cell phone with Roxy, a leading casual apparel, lifestyle brand for young women from the Quiksilver company. The women who buy this phone consider wireless devices a part of their everyday life—a fashion statement and an avenue for self-expression as well as a communication device. Just as Roxy apparel represents freedom, fun and individual expression, so too does the design and custom features of the Roxy–Boost wireless phone manufactured by Motorola.

The Roxy Cell Phone's Gen Y Women-Focused Features

- Ringtones specifically selected with the Roxy girl in mind, including "Funky Town," "Girls Just Wanna Have Fun," "California Dreaming" and "Wake Me Up Before You Go-Go."

- Preloaded Java games, including Tetris and Snood from THQ.

- No credit checks, hidden charges or monthly bills. Boost Mobile customers pay for minutes only as they need them through the purchase of Re-Boost cards.

- Boost 2-Way long-range walkie-talkie feature.

- Built-in speaker phone, 250-entry phonebook, voice-mail, "vibra" call alert.

- National roaming, text messaging and always-on wireless Web access.

**CONNECTING WITH GEN Y WOMEN: LESSONS LEARNED
FROM THE MOBILE PHONE INDUSTRY**

*Position your product within their lifestyle through strategic brand
alliances.* Boost Mobile pursues brand positioning, partnerships, distribution channels, service offerings and price plans, wireless phone
models and other variables that are uniquely suited to the lifestyles
and behaviors of young people.

*Stay on top of technology, continually offering upgrades and increased
access.* Via its mobile Web service, Verizon Wireless is another company positioned to successfully tap the teen segment. By partnering
with Bolt, a global-communications platform for fifteen- to twenty-
year-olds, Verizon will provide mobile Web subscribers access to
"Bolt Everywhere," a wireless platform that enables two-way communications on any WAP-enabled device. Bolt provides proprietary
interactive tools and services that offer teens e-mail, voice mail,
voice chat, people-searching and instant messaging. Now that's
increased access!

Identify and exploit alternative distribution channels. Boost Mobile
phones are available at more than eight hundred locations where
youth prefer to shop, including Best Buy, Wherehouse Music, Good
Guys, Wal-Mart and the wireless and youth fashion retailers where
Roxy and Quiksilver products are sold. Boost Mobile has become an
authentic part of the Gen Y lifestyle culture, by being available
through national retailers, convenience stores and retailers that focus
on music, surf, skate and snow-related activities.

*Offer interactive products that young women can brand with their own
personality.* As we mentioned, the Roxy wireless phone has ring tones
specifically selected for young women by the Roxy design and marketing team. Gen Yers can further personalize their phones by
adding ring tones and graphics that represent their own tastes in
music. They can also download customized content that appeals to

their sports and pop-culture interests. And then there are the additional mobile-related accessories like paste-on nails that illuminate when the phone beeps, hand-set covers, branded carrying cases and mobile desk stands.

Remove payment barriers and provide multiple and flexible options. Boost Mobile's retail channel makes sure there are no credit checks, hidden charges or monthly bills. Their customers pay for minutes only as they need them through the purchase of Re-Boost cards— available in several denominations at locations convenient to a typical youth's day (for example, all authorized Boost Mobile retailers and 7-Eleven stores).

Make wireless Internet easy and highly accessible. Bell Mobility recently transformed its Solo digital-prepaid service into a wireless Web service for its Gen Y segment. Solo subscribers can use their airtime minutes to talk or surf the mobile browser service. Teens can access numerous Web sites, as well as send e-mail, use Yahoo instant messaging, enter concert contests and shop online.

Give Gen Yers the control. This demographic does not respond to hard sell—like inflexible plans, limited phone features, intrusive marketing messages or mobile spamming. Gen Yers need to be empowered to personalize their world and define community building on their own terms.

Generation X Women

The women of Gen X, as you'll see from their key characteristics and the societal transitions that affected them, are harder to label than Gen Y. We won't even try. We'll just give a few guidelines to help you define their perspectives and figure out how their buying minds might view your brand.

There are approximately 30.8 million women between the ages of 24 and 38. The 10.5 million women in the thirty- to thirty-four-year-old age bracket are the largest segment of the young adult Gen X population, accounting for 34 percent of this group.

Perhaps because they emerged as such an unusual or unknown generation, early press coverage routinely described Gen Xers as cynical, distrustful whiners or slackers. The media were wrong and this may have shaped Gen X's mistrust of advertising. Gen X was also smaller in number and didn't get the attention garnered by the larger Baby Boomer and Gen Y populations. However, as they matured and their behavior was further researched and documented, the reputation of these younger adults changed to a more positive, empowered one—more reflective of their true nature—in place of the media spin. In particular, the women of Gen X are now identified as "entrepreneurial, risk-taking, practical, and adaptable."[9] And, that's a long way from whining and slacking off.

GEN X BUYING FILTERS

How can a generation be described as anything from slacker to entrepreneurial and practical? What is unique about this group of young adults whose defining events included Watergate, the 1970s oil crises, the Vietnam War, Roe v. Wade, rising divorce rates, the release of the movie *Star Wars*, the PC revolution and AIDS, among other things? How do their experiences now drive their consumer behavior? Some of the most significant influencers that filter Gen X's views of life include:

Non-traditional upbringing. As the first generation of children whose parents divorced in large numbers, so Gen X was the first era of the latchkey kid. Gen Xers respond to a sense of family and belonging, but not in the traditional nuclear sense. In many cases, their friends have become or replaced their families.

Gender-neutral. Raised by mothers who fought for equality in the workplace, Gen Xers, in general, tend to interact with their peers from a gender-neutral perspective. In particular, Gen X women, as consumers or within the workplace, expect and possibly prefer gender-neutral corporate environments as opposed to overtly female-friendly ones.

Learners. Gen Xers are open to change and growth because that's what they know. They have a true commitment to lifelong education and career development, and they are the first generation where at least 50 percent have high school diplomas. And, being so naturally inclined to learn means they'll lead more entrepreneurial, risk-taking, practical and adaptable lives.

Technology savvy. Because the evolution of home computing paralleled their childhoods and teens, Gen Xers of either gender tend to be extremely comfortable learning technological skills. As part of the front end of the first true Internet generation, these women spent just as much time using computers in childhood or adolescence as did their male peers.

All about "me." Again, because they grew up in a fairly nontraditional culture, Gen Xers didn't, and won't, automatically live their parents' lives. This trend may be especially evident in the way young adult women are enjoying their "me" years. By postponing marriage, enjoying the affluence that comes from high-paying jobs, indulging their whims and buying impulsively, they have broken through the previous generation's mores.

Motherhood on hold. As further evidence of the above, a growing number of women in their early thirties are either postponing or choosing not to have children. Between 1976 and 1998, the percentage of childless thirty- to thirty-four-year-old women increased from 15.6 percent to 27.4 percent.[10]

Professional careers. Given all the other characteristics mentioned in this list, it follows that Gen X women are a significant force in the corporate world. Young adult women are nearly as likely as their male counterparts to hold executive and managerial positions, and they are more likely to be employed in professional positions. Gen Xers, in general, may be less hindered by rules and policies than their parents were, which means they'll find it easier to quit one job and find another, if need be. Finally, even as they delay motherhood and think of themselves as career women, Gen Xers are interested in maintaining a family-work balance when the time does come. They will expect and demand the job flexibility their own mothers couldn't have fathomed.

Financial challenges. Money management is an especially crucial issue for Gen X women. A longer life expectancy and lower lifelong earnings than men make debt one of the biggest sources of stress in the lives of these women in particular. They frequently move in and out of the workforce, reducing their Social Security contributions while increasing their family responsibilities and adding to their personal debt. In general, Gen Xers don't expect to do as well as their parents. These factors suggest that the women of this generation should be extra diligent about saving early, investing aggressively and spending less. (So much for the indulgent "me" years.)

REFLECTING GEN X WOMEN IN YOUR BRAND

Syrupy ad pitches are not the way to reach this resilient and somewhat cynical generation. But hip humor and high-design ad campaigns, like those for the Volkswagen Beetle and Nike's "Just do it" series, have proved quite successful. In fact, many from this generation are likely to be in the ranks of the marketers reading this book. However, if you aren't that of which you seek, it is important to keep a few guidelines in mind when developing a plan to connect young adult Gen X women with your product or service:[11]

Truth in advertising. These women seek real value and will judge companies by how well they honor their promises.

Highly visual. Because of their early exposure to television, Gen X women will likely best respond to visual cues. They prefer less text in advertising and are attuned to Internet-style communication, including e-mail, Web sites and technology-driven media.

Research comes before purchase. Many women in this generation conduct extensive research before making major purchases (they grew up on computers and have been online for a while, after all). That research includes the word-of-mouth they hear from friends and family and what they read online, whether in your marketing materials or in discussion groups.

Ever-changing and upgrading. Unlike older generations, young adult women tend to switch brands often and do what they can to keep up with new styles. The "freshness" factor is key when you are trying to reach this market with new product designs or marketing campaigns.

The environment matters. Generation X has taken what they've discovered about recycling and environmentally safe products and applied it throughout their lives and to their buying behavior. In fact, Simmons Market Research Bureau found that, starting at the age of 18, all women are more likely to buy products in recycled-paper packaging.[12] Gen Xers are also quick to notice whether the products they buy have been animal tested.

Gender-neutral modus operandi. Opting for inclusive rather than exclusive treatment makes the most sense for this group. Just as with Gen Y women, overtly female-focused marketing efforts for non-gender-specific products or services will fall flat.

GEN X INDUSTRY STUDY: BUYING, DECORATING, AND TRADING SPACES

Members of Gen X are moving into their peak earning and spending years, and are rapidly settling into new living spaces. Long-term relationships, marriage and decisions to start a family have all combined with lower interest rates to make home, loft or apartment ownership more logical and attainable.

This generation is being inspired and courted by a growing roster of established retailers, manufacturers, television and cable shows, and magazines whose executives have realized that late twenty- and early thirty-somethings want to create homes that don't look or feel anything like their parent's home.

---

gen x home decor case study: crate & barrel's offshoot, cb2

With children of Boomers their core consumers, the CB2 store managers strive for a hip and casual style, using lots of alternative materials and edgier designs. There is much more color and much more attention to home office needs and much less emphasis on gourmet cooking. (Generation X remains big on eating out.)

The CB2 store's whole presentation is thus heavily skewed toward the Gen X customer—from its location in a rapidly gentrifying urban neighborhood near Chicago's Wrigley Field to the pulsing techno grooves playing in the background.

The CB2 shopper is a youngish urban professional (age 25–40) who is highly mobile and, thus, very interested in tech gadgets. These hip people are trendy, yes, but they still shy away from gimmicks.

Crate & Barrel anticipated the needs of Gen X and began to develop the CB2 concept in the mid-1990s. Having been in business with loyal customers for some forty years, Crate & Barrel knew it had to tap into the next generational wave in order to stay on trend and attract the sons and daughters of their established customers.[13]

Retail stores like CB2 (see sidebar); Pottery Barn's West Elm, a catalogue-only operation aimed at attracting customers ages 24 to 39; and EQ3, the offshoot of Manitoba, Canada–based Palliser Furniture, are all tapping into this Gen X-rooted boom in hip and cost-effective home styling. This generation has also fueled the success of cable and television shows like The Learning Channel's *Trading Spaces*. Not only has *Trading Spaces* started a whole clan of new spin-offs, but other channels have also jumped on the fun and stylish fixer-upper bandwagon with shows like TBS's *House Rules*, a remodeling reality competition, and Home & Garden Television's planned show called *What Have I Done?!*

CONNECTING WITH GEN X WOMEN: LESSONS FROM THE HOME DECORATION INDUSTRY

First, Gen X customers want good value with style, not low-quality household merchandise. They like to take the fun, funky and celebrity home styles they see on television and in movies and magazines and translate them into things they can afford.

They have higher expectations and are looking for a more stimulating, ever-changing and entertaining shopping experience. For this generation, decorating their space often falls into the entertainment and fashion category; so their budgets for home furnishing and design could well compete with trips to Starbucks, personal accessories, movie tickets and other entertainment. For this group of shoppers, an olive green shag ottoman might be as expressive, fun and emotionally satisfying to purchase as a hip techno-gadget like the iPod.

Finally, lifestyles are different for urban Gen X women. Many of them are career professionals who have chosen to settle into an urban loft, apartment or townhouse, rather than into a sprawling spread in the suburbs from which to commute to work. Thus, these urban women will have very different storage, furniture and decorating needs and preferences than their suburban counterparts.

Baby Boom Women

Born between 1945 and 1964, the Baby Boom generation (a.k.a. Boomers), are approximately 80.2 million strong and represent over a quarter of the total U.S. population. Every year, starting in 1996, over four million members of this group reach age 50—and this wave will continue for the next decade. With the biggest monetary advantages of any generation in history, and their ensuing demand for new products and services, the over-50 market is hugely impacting every industry.

As with Gen X, no single label fits the Boomer group, mainly because its members were born over such a wide span of eventful years. The Cold War, the introduction and development of television, the Kennedy assassination, the Beatles, the Vietnam War and Watergate are just a few of the defining events of this generation's formative years.

Of the generations represented in society today, Boomers have lived during some extremely exciting transition years. More than twice as many of these women graduated from college by age 24 than did their predecessors; and more Boomer women work than women of either generation before or after. Furthermore, research by Allstate Financial in 2003 revealed that, as the large generation of Boomer women moves toward traditional retirement age, 71 percent of all Boomers don't expect to ever stop working completely. Interestingly, that study showed that women were more likely to say they'll keep working for the social interactions, whereas men for the job satisfaction.

The introduction of the birth control pill in 1960 enabled Boomer women, in general, to postpone marriage until their mid-twenties or beyond. Because many of this generation delayed marriage and then experienced high divorce rates, a large number of them have lived independently for years. In fact, while Boomers have been the most divorced generation, they were also the generation that made the two-income household a norm.[14] These go-getter women are used to keeping their own homes, managing their own money and tending to emergencies by themselves.

BABY BOOMERS' BUYING FILTERS

The industrious women of the Baby Boom generation have staked their claim and are living full and very different lives from their parents. Few of these women are stay-at-homes, and the world is probably a better place for their gumption. Some specific Boomer characteristics that filter their view of life include:

Interests, not age. These women are restless and won't be defined by age alone. As Boomer women get older and their grown children leave home, their health and vitality, creativity, family and friends, and work and avocation take on even more importance. They feel there are too many fun and exciting things left to do!

Stressed and time-starved. Given all their roles and interests—from holding professional careers to managing mom duties and carrying the bulk of household and childrearing responsibilities—these women could easily be the most stressed-out group in America. Yet, they survive because of another Boomer characteristic: a concern for their own health and a willingness to spend time and money on their personal needs.

Caregiving. Many Boomer women are simultaneously taking care of elderly parents and their children. One statistic estimates that Boomers will spend about the same number of years caring for their parents as they spend rearing their children! Furthermore, most Boomer women (ages 39–54, in particular), agree that their kids have a significant impact on the brands they buy.[15]

Confident and optimistic. Many professional Boomer women say that fifty feels like an optimistic, can-do stage of life. They are establishing second careers or using virtual offices and computer technology to reinvent the common perceptions of retirement.

Active and healthy. Boomer women tend to feel younger and are likely to live longer than the women of any previous generation. They seek rejuvenation and relaxation and will come up with the cash to get it. Many women in this group exercise daily, have regular massages and practice meditation or yoga, for example. In fact, the November 2001 issue of *American Demographics* reported that 55 percent of current health club members (or about eighteen million) were forty or older.

REFLECTING BOOMER WOMEN IN YOUR BRAND

Make no assumptions about this active and tradition-challenging group of women. Valuing self-fulfillment, self-improvement and self-empowerment, Boomer women have been doing their own thing for years.

Interestingly, aging Boomer women who we might think had long since settled on their brands of choice may not be as loyal as we supposed. In fact, one report found that even as brand loyalty was eroding across all age segments, the steepest drops were occurring among older consumers.[16] So, you'll need to stay on your toes and take nothing for granted about this group.

Some key truths to remember in crafting marketing messages that will land within a Boomer woman's field of vision include:

Forget senior discounts. Many of the older Boomer women feel that "senior discounts" or "mature" pitches don't apply to them. The women in this age group will continue to deny the number and instead seek products that reflect how young they still feel. You'll need to find a new way to provide a discount that doesn't remind these women of their silver hair.

Support connectedness. A sense of purpose is imperative to Boomer women, and they see any power they've developed in their lives as a tool for sharing with peers or for pursuing their own more socially connected goals.

Promote youthful appearance. Products will strike a resonant chord that support youthful appearance and physical upkeep for female Boomers, without going overboard on beauty for beauty's sake. Whether we like it or not, women more than men are generally judged on appearance, so maintaining a youthful vibrancy through the onset of menopausal physical changes is important to Boomer women.

Be a knowledge source. Present the inside scoop to this segment of women and be loved for it. The more knowledge Boomer women have, the more empowered they feel, and the more confident they will be to try new products and explore new industries.

Get to the point. Keep ads and direct mail short and sweet. Boomer women are grateful to companies whose marketing copy first establishes a benefit and a need and only then proceeds to a comprehensive pitch. Whether through your Web site, catalog or toll-free number, enable these busy, knowledgeable women to quickly obtain information and order your products day or night.

BABY BOOM INDUSTRY STUDY: PERSONAL GROWTH

Baby Boom women are fueling an enormous personal development industry that covers all areas of life, from finances, health, and career to spirituality and food. The more successful personal growth brands that serve Boomer women tend to be anchored by a key expert or personality. This spokesperson can become more real and more relevant in women's lives through a multichanneled, integrated marketing approach that includes books, magazines, syndicated columns, TV and radio shows, personal tours and e-newsletters.

Oprah Winfrey is the epitome of personal growth leaders, as we all couldn't help but notice. Starting out as a traditional talk show host in the 1980s, she has since become a huge influence on women, particularly on Boomers' self-development. Yet, she has also used her success to expand that reach. Through her television show

(*Oprah*), magazine (*O, The Oprah Magazine*), Web site, and personal tours, Oprah has enlisted emerging leaders from a variety of fields to deliver their expertise to her audience and subscribers.

Touted as "The women's personal growth guide for the new century," *O* magazine well represents Oprah's relationships with these experts. The magazine's roster of columnists include: financial guru Suze Orman on how emotions affect personal finances; self-help author Phillip McGraw, Ph.D., on relationships; Julie Morgenstern on getting organized in every area of life; Martha Beck on personal life coaching; and the radio airwave's Satellite Sisters, who provide five different perspectives on random topics. Oprah has single-handedly (along with her large staff) simplified the personal growth industry by collecting together the finest experts into a one-stop resource for women seeking that help in their lives.

CONNECTING WITH BOOMER WOMEN: LESSONS FROM OPRAH WINFREY

The overall success of Oprah's television show, Web site and magazine derives from the authentic human tone they take in delivering information that almost every woman, and many men, can use. A few more specific lessons to learn from Oprah are:

Staff up with members of the community you serve. Oprah's media empire is an excellent example of a brand that succeeded because the founders and staff were themselves members of the community to which they catered. Oprah's staff of Boomers and older Gen Xers regularly gather to discuss what is top of mind in their own lives, and often these issues are the very ones that are most relevant for their audience.

Stay close to your audience and include them in the story. Oprah's staff keep their fingers on the pulse of their audience using e-mail and their Web site. The Web site section "Be on the show" lists show topics that are currently in development and invites audience members to share their own stories and insights about these topics. Those who e-mail in their personal stories are often included in the program and asked to join the audience for the day.

People connect with people, not programs. Give a face to some of life's most challenging topics by developing expert personalities and using them to educate the masses. Keep the content specific and the language relatable, and deliver the information in the context of real lives.

Dialogue and conversation are crucial. Oprah and her staff have taken the lid off virtually all topics formerly taboo with their audiences. Oprah and her staff are ready to connect, relate, discuss and solve problems. The key to maintaining the dialogue among women is to condense the discussion and make it fun, without taking them for extended periods away from the other demands of their lives. Personal coach Cheryl Richardson, author of *Life Makeovers* and frequent guest on Oprah, has developed a great example of this in action: Her Web site, Cherylrichardson.com, has registered over one thousand "LM [Life Makeover] Groups," whose members meet in person to discuss the topics in Richardson's books and newsletters.[17]

Integrate your channels and understand your market's comfort level with technology. Oprah's Web site is evidence that her team understands something simple that a lot of other content companies have missed: Many Boomer women do not have the Internet bandwidth or the patience to watch a video clip online. Instead Oprah offers content from her TV shows in quick, easy-access slide shows.

Mature Women

The Mature market demographic spans thirty years or more, a huge group that deserves your undivided attention. While people age 50 and older (about 81 million strong) account for only 28 percent of the population, they represent nearly 50 percent of total consumer demand, 65 percent of total net worth and 70 percent of all personal financial assets.[18] And, with some 31 million of the Baby Boomers we just discussed having already turned fifty by 2003, we have all the more incentive to learn to serve aging consumers well.

As women mature (and in direct contrast to younger consumers), they realize their economic power, get more active, and let go of more of their cares. They are waiting much longer to retire and have figured out what they need to do to keep feeling ten to fifteen years younger.

Within the vast Mature market, diverse attitudes and behaviors abound. Separated by decades in some cases, members of this group were born in different time periods with their lives and attitudes shaped by distinct events—from World War II to the postwar flight to the suburbs to the Beat movement and the Korean War (and you can throw in the phenomenon of Elvis Presley, too).

It would be inconceivable to stereotype anyone who was born and raised in this era. Rather, to best understand them and the way they may see the world and the brands they purchase, we have to thoroughly examine mindsets, life stages and lifestyles.

That said, Mature Americans can be broken into three different blocks that are defined roughly by age, with corresponding mind-set and lifestyle factors, which include:

Pre-retirees (Ages 56–65). This particular block of older Boomers and younger Matures has reached an empty-nesting stage and many have already become grandparents. Preretirees are still quite active and busy, but are starting to wind down and prepare for the next stage of their lives. Because many remain in the workforce, they continue to earn and consume. With responsibilities decreasing, more of the expenditures of people in this group can be self-directed and self-satisfying.

Active Retirees (Ages 66–75). These women are living full lives that include plenty of recreation, travel, friendships, adult education, grandparenting, hobbies and business interests. However, many are also beginning to experience health issues that need to be actively managed.

Seniors (Age 76+). Although their pace of life has slowed considerably, due to a likely decline in physical health, many of these older adults are still interested in being social and using their minds. Others may have reached a stage in their lives where they no longer can live independently and so require the help of a caregiver. It's worth noting that the fastest growing segment of the U.S. population today includes those who are over age 85.[19]

MATURE WOMEN'S BUYING FILTERS

In addition to the specific age-ranges within the Mature segment, there are different sets of values, outside events, and levels of technology that influence their consumer behavior. Those non-mutually-exclusive categories can be described as follows:

Selectively indulgent. Women in this Mature market subgroup have lived in good economic times and many feel they have earned the right to indulge by buying top-quality or big-ticket items.

Aides and collaborators. Women of this era have given much time to volunteer efforts that have advanced women's rights and achieved other significant cultural benchmarks. They "have been pioneers in civil rights, consumer activism and feminism, but they have often gone unrecognized for these roles."[20]

Internet embracers. The Mature market, in general, is the fastest growing group on the Internet. Nielsen NetRatings found that from October 2002 to October 2003 the number of Matures 65 and older online surged 25 percent, to 9.6 million surfers—representing 7 percent of the online population.[21] Industry estimates are that by 2010 about 70 percent of seniors will be using the Internet.[22] There seems to be boundless opportunity for reaching and serving these elder Internet enthusiasts.

Energetic and active. Medical advances have extended the length of middle age, and these women see themselves as vibrant and full of life, not old. "Aging" is a dirty word, so many of the women in this group regularly buy hair color and use products that safely overcome the typical body and health changes that come with the additional years.

REFLECTING MATURE WOMEN IN YOUR BRAND

If you want to reach these women of a "certain age," be careful to craft marketing messages that aren't overly trendy, but rather demonstrate an understanding of their position in life as grandparents, active travelers and high-energy learners. Speak to their lifestyle, not to their age.

The great complaint by many older women is that, indeed, marketers seem to think that by the time you achieve senior status—and in some movie theaters, that's 60!—you've lost interest in clothing altogether.

—Tam Gray, founder and editor of Seniorwomen.com

Furthermore, just as you should consider the ages of your marketing team when marketing to other generations of women, you also need to get the Mature perspective from within when you are trying to reach this older market. In its 2002 publication, *Marketing to the 50-Plus Population*, the editors at EPM Communications found that, "Young marketers are at a loss about how to target older adults, and so end up pitching their products to themselves, since it's what they know best."[23] So, a good thing to remember when building marketing teams to reach any segment is to make sure you are representative, however you can, of the demographic you seek.

Given the latter overarching guideline, there are a few common traits of Mature generation women that should be reflected in your brand, including that these women:

Look to experts. Unlike Boomers, these women respond more favorably to authority figures and value the opinions of industry experts. They tend to consult their doctors and look for seals of approval and other signs of official endorsement whenever they encounter an unfamiliar health concern, brand or industry.

Resent age-related adjectives. Descriptive terms like "golden" and "twilight" cause offense and are likely to miss the mark. Especially when the goal is to resonate with the women of the Mature market, a marketing message should address a certain value or interest instead of blindly speaking to an age range.

Build human connection via interactivity. Mature women appreciate being asked for feedback and like to feel as though they are part of a larger community.

Appreciate the personalized approach. Mature adults value feeling known and recognized, so it is worth the effort to customize a mass-market message, especially when delivered via e-mail or the Internet.

Use intuition and tap into emotion. Experts say that the way people process information changes as we age. As people get older, the intuitive and holistic thinking of the right brain begins to take precedence over the left brain's more linear and logical form of thinking. Given this change in brain processing, it may be most effective to reach Mature women by appealing to their emotions first, and then providing the data and facts about your product further along in their buying process.

Are focused on their life stage, not their age. In the decade between ages 50 and 60, people experience more life transitions—like the birth of a grandchild, remarriage or the death of a parent—than in any other decade of life. Going through such an intense transitional period brings about a strong focus on these matters, while the age filter fades even further into the background of their decision making.

Seek an enhanced, active lifestyle. With increases in free time and disposable income, older consumers look for products and services that will enhance their lifestyles and not those that prepare them for slowing down or settling in.

MATURES INDUSTRY STUDY: ACTIVE TRAVEL

The women of today's Mature market represent an enormous opportunity and challenge. Though they are aging, the women of this generation generally remain no less active. In fact, grandparents today are younger (the average age for becoming a grandparent for the first time is 47), wealthier and in better health today than at any time previously; and their spending is growing about 10 percent a year.[24] Enter, stage right, the active travel and tour industry.

From radio segments like Public Radio International's "Savvy Traveler" (part of PRI's *Marketplace*) to retailers like TravelSmith and Web sites like Poshnosh.com and SeniorCycling.com, many businesses in the active travel industry have developed to serve mature travelers, the fastest growing group of consumers in this industry.

In fact, a 2000 study conducted by the Travel Industry Association found that Matures comprise nearly one-third of all U.S. travelers, and that these elder adventurers are wealthier, more educated and more technologically savvy than they had been even five years before.[25] Furthermore, Mature generation travelers stay on the road longer and tend to take longer trips (3.9 nights), compared with 3.4 nights on average for travelers overall.

In general, travelers who are age 55 and over are nearly twice as likely to participate in tours as those in other age groups. And, many of these active group travelers are women who have gained independence and become involved in more adventurous activities after the death of a spouse.

They may not match the mileage of their younger counterparts or sleep in tents, but Mature women tend to be in good shape and can enjoy themselves. In general, they have the money, energy and brainpower to take on new interests and to continue to enthusiastically engage in life. They look for trips that provide both intellectual stimulation and access to interesting people.

SavvyTraveler.org, the Web site companion to the "Savvy Traveler" segment on PRI's *Marketplace*, is an example of how to serve Mature generation women travelers well. In addition to providing audio versions of archived stories on exotic journeys or on the usual destinations but with a new twist, the Web site includes a library, a "Traveler's Aid" section (which covered how to avoid a rental car fiasco the day we checked it) and an extensive "Traveler's Toolbox." From maps to language tips to help with visas, passports and emergency services abroad (in addition to the usual information on planes, trains and travel agents), this section on its own is a true resource. Though not presented as such, the information on SavvyTraveler.org with its simple and direct navigation speaks to a Mature generation's travel issues (without alienating any other market segment).

Other examples of companies that appeal to the Mature generation travel market are TravelSmith, a travelwear online and catalog retailer; SeniorCycling.com, a bike touring company geared toward the over-50 market; and Poshnosh.com, the Web site run by Senior Women's Travel that focuses on culinary experiences, literary connections (great writers and their relationships to each city), unique sightseeing and great shopping. (Where do we sign up?) Whether they specifically focus on women or not, these companies have all developed product lines or information resources delivered in ways that effectively serve Mature women travelers.

CONNECTING WITH MATURE WOMEN: LESSONS FROM THE TRAVEL INDUSTRY

Learning from the successes in the travel industry in effectively reaching women of the Mature generation can improve your marketing to this important demographic.

Prepare for a wide variety of interests. Mature travel consumers are no longer just calling the travel agent to book a cruise. They want to plan and explore the travel possibilities for themselves. They are heading online and considering options that might include active trips by bike, kayak and foot, or slightly more passive trips to ever-more exotic places—like the Galapagos Islands and Tibet. Mature women enjoy the whole process from pretrip research to the actual adventure, so travel-related companies should provide as many options, presented in as many different ways, as they can.

Deliver relevant images, content and testimonials. Relevance comes in many varieties, as these travel industry examples reflect: The Poshnosh.com site has packaged tours such as grandchild trips and family celebrations; and the SavvyTraveler.com "Tool Box" includes links and resources for getting along while you're there as well as a section on who to call to fix things that might go wrong (links to the U.S. Embassy directory and to the Centers for Disease Control are two examples).

Don't make assumptions. Knitting needles are rusting in their baskets as the Mature generation women of today take off to cycle the Italian countryside or explore Mexico with friends and companions. The travel-related companies and Web sites we mention have learned to see their market through the perspective of a thriving, life-experienced generation, many of whom are women. The destinations highlighted, the clothing presented and the resources listed therein show that the travel industry has been digging more deeply to discover and serve the needs and interests of its Mature generation travelers. And, it's gone way beyond the cruises, one-size-fits-all outfits and travel agent phone numbers of years past.

Conclusion: The Generational Foundations of a Woman's Buying Mind

Before your brand can even begin to reflect the perspectives of the women it serves, you have to understand the societal and cultural influences that have taken hold of them. Whatever extra effort you expend in order to learn about and understand the general com-monalities of the women in your market will become clear in the way you present your product or service. And, this is a good thing.

Women of all generations seek a connection with those brands that seem to authentically understand them. By doing the home-work to thoroughly comprehend the events and realities that have shaped these generations, you can more clearly see the nature of each woman's natural buying inclinations. From there, adding and taking away the filters of a woman's life transitions and roles, among other things, will produce a much more accurate place from which to build your new consumer connection.

CHAPTER 6

looking beyond generations

the buying filters of life stages and roles

THOUGH THE QUICKEST way to segment the women's market may be by generation, the common cross-generational traits and
roles a woman plays in the course of her life may carry even more
weight. The unplanned-for circumstances and life experiences of the
here and now may more directly affect a woman's buying needs. For
example, although she may have been born into Generation X, her
most immediate needs may be all about taking care of her kids or
heading up her own business.

When a brand's products and services support a woman's prime
focus of the day—her children, her career, the elder she cares for

or her workout at the gym—they reflect an awareness of the life stages and extenuating circumstances in her life.

For example, just imagine a group of today's mothers dropping off their children for preschool: some are age 45 and some are 28, some are running off to work and others are stay-at-homes, but their mommy life stage gives them more in common than not. When women are in the mom stage, you are less likely to tempt them with spontaneous travel opportunities or gourmet cooking clubs, because their focus is their kids (and their health, college tuition and so on)—the time demands of which preclude many luxuries.

The shared emotions and concerns of moms can be described as one big filter through which they see everything during that particular life stage: products, ad campaigns and your company's social causes.

In this chapter, we'll explore a few key life stages for women and then go into the possible array of roles they might play in a lifetime (or even in a single day). It's fascinating to consider how many seemingly unrelated things can affect their consumer purchases, or filter their buying minds.

SINGLE WOMEN, BUSINESSWOMEN AND MOMS

Single women, businesswomen and moms may span ages from teens to late fifties, and beyond. And, women may experience two life stages concurrently, if they choose to maintain their jobs while they raise their families, for example. Or, singlehood may be the life stage that currently takes precedence and more significantly influences their buying behavior than does their career. You just can't predict.

So, in order to reach women in these roles, you need to deliver products and services that represent convenience, ease-of-use and reliability. We've got an easy mantra for you to keep in mind when trying to connect with any women in the single women, business-women and moms roles: "Make their lives easier."

Let's focus in on those three groups—single women, busi-nesswomen and moms—and then consider ways to ensure that women, in whatever life stages or roles, see your brand as part of their lives.

Single Women

Though in years past the solo phase in a woman's life may have been a short one . . . my, how things have changed.

Due to a variety of contemporary social trends—including greater career opportunities for women, higher divorce rates and longer life expectancy—women today are simply spending more periods of their lives living solo. While "single" was once the term reserved mainly for the time between a woman's schooling and inevitable marriage, the word now covers the series of living-alone stages that occur randomly over the course of a woman's extra long life (research shows that women now live six or more years longer than men).

In fact, U.S. Census Bureau data indicated that in 2001 there were over 17 million women living alone, which was more than double the number of women living alone twenty years before.

Part of the reason for that growing number of solo women over-all is that there has been a steady decline in the rate of marriages over the past thirty or so years, with 55 percent of adult women married in 1998, down from 66 percent in 1960.[1] And, this chang-ing marriage rate coincides with an increase in women's education levels and their participation in the commercial workforce.[2]

While some of these women have experienced some years in marriage, many never take that step at all these days. Some single women co-habit with male or female partners and some share group houses in a "family" made of friends. The Census Bureau more formally segments the "unmarried women" (with or without children) into the following subgroups: never married, separated, divorced and widowed.

With all those variables to consider, single women remain well worth pursuing as a consumer market. They are poised to become one of the most influential economic forces of this century, with the aggregate solo female income estimated to reach $199.3 billion in 2006, up 20 percent from 2001.[3] Other single lifestyle trends to keep in mind include:

□ Women living solo are, for the most part, content and in control. These women don't see their status as a rejection of the concept of marriage, but rather a refusal to bargain away elements of their lifestyles in exchange for a partnership. Whether they are heterosexual or lesbian, these women are often single by choice.

□ They intentionally take on motherhood without a partner. With more women marrying later in life or choosing to remain single forever, it is becoming more common for solo women to have children outside of marriage. Some women in this segment may simply consider motherhood a part of their self-fulfillment. This motherhood on their terms will demand a very different marketing appeal from that used to reach traditional moms.

□ They have unconventional living arrangements. Single women are creating lifestyles that work for them as individuals, paying little attention to how they "ought to" do things. Of course, where and how a single woman chooses to live can have a dramatic impact on the marketplace. Here are a few examples to consider:[4]

– Single women who live in urban areas fuel leisure and entertainment spending.

– Suburbanite single women fuel the multibillion dollar hardware and home improvement industry.

– Singles living with their parents spend their disposable income on whatever pleases them most.

THE BUYING FILTERS OF SINGLE WOMEN

A single woman's distinct identities, aspirations and modes of consumption will be key filters through which she sees your brand. With many in the solo group focusing on the positive aspects of their lives, they are driven to pursue mental and physical self-development, and your marketing approach should reflect that. Blow that "spinster" stereotype out of the water! (But, also keep in mind that not everyone resembles the Carrie Bradshaw character in HBO's popular series *Sex and the City*.)

A single woman today will tap into her circle of friends for purchasing advice as well as for social activities and travel. Marketers should pay close attention to how and why single women connect through these networks, and be aware of the ways solo women will regularly take a friend's advice over anything (including your advertising messages).

A few more details of the life filters through which single women may see your brand include:

Family redefined. As marriage rates plunge, community and friendship have become ever more important for single women. "Family" has taken on a whole new meaning for them and may include friends, pets and even online communities, as well as their blood relatives.[5] Perhaps as a way to fill any nuclear family gap, women are now gathering around numerous and more diverse common interests, from Pilates classes to book clubs, cycling groups or investment gatherings.

Healthy lifestyles. To begin with, many single women are avid exercisers and proactive health consumers. Even in the midst of their busy schedules, they still tend to have more time for such pursuits than their coupled or married friends. But beyond the fitness and health

interests, single women have time (in general) to more often participate in activities like adventure travel, outdoor sports and movie-
going. These women will certainly notice the products and services
that fuel their active lifestyles in a healthy and convenient way.

Living a spiritual journey. For some single women, personal development means improving the spirit as well as the body and mind.
Their personal spiritual practices may emphasize introspection or
a formal religion, but single women are also taking advantage of
educational opportunities to attain personal fulfillment such as
reading books and magazines, attending seminars and retreats and
forming spiritually based groups.

Empowered, not waiting. Single women are often more than happy
to settle into their lives long before they find a husband or life partner. They purchase typical bridal registry items such as china, furniture, appliances and other bigger-ticket household products—all
for themselves.

REFLECTING SINGLE WOMEN IN YOUR BRAND

As with other segments of the women's market, single women are
looking for fair treatment, improved standards of service and products or services that demonstrate a respect and understanding of
their viewpoints. The most effective marketing messages will be
those that reflect their intelligence, honor their myriad lifestyle
choices and affirm their self-esteem and independent spirit.

Industry-Specific Tips for Reaching Single Women

Consumer packaged goods. Smaller portioned groceries as well as
products that more specifically highlight the health concerns of
women are in great demand by singles. For example, functional
foods with soy, calcium and organic ingredients strongly mirror a
single woman's healthy and empowered lifestyle.

Real estate. Homes that particularly cater to a single woman's priorities, and are insightfully designed and built, will likely become more popular. For example, adjoining residences for single women and partners and friends who wish to live nearby, but not with one another, should sell well. In addition, homes that focus their square footage and building budget on the main living areas (not extra bedrooms) will suit many solo lifestyles. And, in general, the current small-house trend will be especially significant among women strongly motivated by environmental, community and social causes.

Travel. With such typically fast-paced and highly active daily lives, single women are also more likely to approach travel in the same way. This group of women, young or old, have become a major influence on the further emergence of the adventure travel industry. Single women demonstrate their active and empowered traits by networking with other women to make group plans or to travel together for safety reasons. They will then take their community of travel a step further by sharing their experiences in support and encouragement of one another's future journeys. For example, Journeywoman.com is an online community "by women and for women" that presents travel through the eyes of empowered and active women, many of whom are single.

Entrepreneurship. Single women with vim, vigor, ideas and money are helping shape how business will be conducted from here on out. They are forming their own companies, and evolving into a class of telecommuting employees and entrepreneurs that demand flexible schedules and decision-making authority.

SINGLE-WOMEN-FOCUSED INDUSTRY STUDY: SNACKS AND SMALL PORTION MEALS

More Americans are living by themselves and are losing their interest in preparing food: It just doesn't seem worth it when they will be the only ones eating. The food industry has monitored this trend and has resized and repackaged many items to better serve the solo household.

Single women, in particular, who tend to seek healthy options in the prepackaged food they buy, seem to have fueled the industry. The ever-popular prewashed salad greens in a bag, for example, were one of the first packaging innovations to really serve women (single or not). Now, perhaps that product should be fine-tuned to half portions, because the reality is that the second half often goes to waste. Following are a few ways the packaged and snack food industry has responded to the particular needs of single women:

□ *Snacks, instead of meals.* Whether it's the healthiest choice or not, the daily diets of many single women often include more snacks than traditional meals. In the course of their workdays and packed social schedules, eating has become more an afterthought (as in "Gee, I forgot to eat a real meal today") or just a quick response to sudden hunger.

As this societal trend takes over, grazing or snacking has gained social acceptance, as a way to meet daily caloric and nutritional needs. Health and nutrition magazines are also touting the benefits of eating five or six smaller meals, as a way to more evenly fuel a human body over the course of a day, as opposed to going longer periods between three larger meals. Furthermore, the increasing time pressures on U.S. consumers, driven by longer working and commuting hours in many cases, are another reason people aren't pausing for the luxury of a full-course meal.

□ *Portable foods.* As the number of meals eaten outside the home has increased, consumer desire for easy-to-prepare food has led to strong growth in snack bars, meal replacement drinks, and frozen and chilled food—or anything that can possibly be eaten with one hand. Snack bars, which are often in the form of high-protein energy bars, are a convenient meal replacement that requires no cooking or utensils. Energy bars, in particular, offer the full complement of nutrients that women, in particular, desire—and all within a small portable package.

Luna Bars (a division of Clif Bar, Inc.) are energy bars that have become a staple for many women we know. Each bar contains the full complement of women-specific nutrients and tastes good! As evidenced by the content on their Web site and the events they sponsor, the company effectively connects with its women customers by marketing in authentic ways as well.

□ *Single servings.* For those consumers who want more variety in their portable eating, single-serve packages of products like Lean Pockets, milk and cereal bars are filling the need. Frito-Lay thought of it all by presenting "Go-Snacks," a serving of savory snacks in a crush-proof, resealable plastic container that fits in a car's cup holder. Along those same lines, Campbell Soup has introduced a portable, microwaveable canned soup called "Soup at Hand," developed to allow consumers to sip soup from one hand while out and about.

Partially prepared foods that require just a few added ingredients to create a one plate meal, and the ultragourmet salad bars that also offer a variety of main and side dishes, are a few more ways that brands, grocery stores and fast food outlets are heeding the snacking and mobile meal-time needs of the single women consumer.

Businesswomen

Workingwomen and female entrepreneurs, who together comprise the businesswomen market, wield mighty economic influence today. And the effect of that economic influence can be felt in both the business and nonbusiness realms. What women learn in making business purchases will likely be incorporated into their off-hour buying behavior. As holistically minded as most women are, it would be difficult to differentiate their personal consumer buying knowledge from their business consumer experiences.

The heavily consuming groups of businesswomen and moms frequently overlap in age ranges and certain characteristics, and they often do both "jobs" simultaneously. Given their time constraints and need to quickly gather health and family information, the Internet came into common use none too soon for the women living this duality. We'll start by taking a particularly close look at businesswomen and how to reflect their needs through online marketing efforts.

Within the businesswomen market segment, women who own businesses and female entrepreneurs, as opposed to workingwomen in general, are becoming an even more powerful market segment with every year. In fact, when you specifically examine the segment in the United States of privately held women-owned firms (where at least 50 percent of the ownerships is female), you see some incredible numbers. As of 2002, there were 3.9 million privately held 50 percent women-owned businesses, employing about 9 million workers, and generating $1.17 trillion in sales.[6] Of these firms, over 166,000 have revenues of at least $1 million and about 6,900 have one hundred or more employees. The largest concentration of these firms is in the service sector, followed by retail, construction, finance, real estate and insurance.

BUSINESSWOMEN'S BUYING FILTERS

Most workingwomen juggle an array of responsibilities and want to quickly extract the essence from important topics in order to make buying decisions for work and home. Just as making lives easier is a good tip for marketing to single women, so is it a good rule of thumb for businesswomen (who may also be single, we know). The difference is that marketing to women in their business roles puts your brand top of mind for their personal purchases as well. Serve one role well and capture her attention for the purchases she makes in her other roles.

Since women, as business owners or in other roles, are likely to conduct exhaustive advance research on significant purchases via independent sites, why not establish your brand or site as their one-stop resource? For example, if your brand risks providing third-party product reviews to support their prebuying behavior, these women will learn to head to your site first when making their next purchase, for business or personal use. This feature could look like a matrix comparing the features and benefits of the top brands in your industry, or a comprehensive checklist helping customers think through the variables involved in the purchase.

In addition, the relationship-building characteristic of most women will likely affect their business habits as well. Take vendor selection, for example: As a relationship-minded woman considers her hiring or buying, she will be more likely than male entrepreneurs to seek advice from associates and advisors, and she will place more emphasis on vendor quality, service and reputation.[7]

In addition to seeking quality over price, a few more purchase influencers for businesswomen include:

▫ Brand loyalty

▫ Desire for customer service and training

▫ Value of efficient Web sites

Overall, the way these very busy women purchase goods and services seems to reflect a tendency toward efficiency combined with social awareness. Other shared characteristics of businesswomen include:

Combine business and personal buying. Eighty percent of women employees and 74 percent of women business owners say that they typically combine business and personal errands or tasks in a single shopping trip.[8] To better serve a businesswoman's efficient buying tendency, for example, brands may consider expanding inventories to include products (personal and bulk portions) and services (express shipping and postage) that fit both categories of items on a woman's shopping list.

Influenced by environmental and social responsibility. For business-women—entrepreneurs and employees alike—the environmental friendliness of a product exerts a major influence on their consumer purchasing decisions. Many of these women also agree that the social responsibility of the company offering the product or service is a major influence on their decision to buy or not.

Hiring help. Given their focus on saving time, it is no surprise that women business owners are more likely to contract for house-cleaning and lawn services. Workingwomen, in general, seem to be finding it easier to let go of the superwoman ideal, admit they need help and feel empowered to get it.

REFLECTING BUSINESSWOMEN IN YOUR BRAND

Workingwomen seem more likely to take shopping cues from their business realms into their personal realms, than the reverse. For example, a woman who becomes accustomed to subcontracting her graphic design needs for business may then be that much more likely to realize the benefit and stress-relief of hiring out yard or housecleaning jobs.

How can marketing messages be developed to incorporate these clues to a businesswoman's buying behavior? A few ideas include:

▫ *Promote the quality and advantages of your product or service first.* The price seems to carry a bit less weight for workingwomen.

▫ *Develop products that can be used in both businesses and households to leverage the brand loyalty of a businesswoman.* This may mean repackaging the product or offering different sizes for each use. Costco and other warehouse retailers have successfully embraced the concept. In the past you would buy a huge box of corn flakes, and by the time you finished it you were sick of them. Now three different standard sizes (often with different flavors) are bundled into a single variety pack—which allows customers to buy in bulk, but the packages are easy to divide and share.

□ *Offer product training with a personal touch.* Perhaps because working women may be a bit less inclined to take the time to study an instruction manual, they consistently rank tech support and customer service as high priorities when choosing vendors. So, offer as much training and coaching as possible, and then be sure to promote that benefit in your marketing materials.

□ *Provide ways to speed through a purchase.* Both online and off, many businesswomen are inclined to be speedy shoppers.

□ *Present full- and fast-service Web sites.* Sites that will resonate deeply with businesswomen have quickly loading pages, resource sections with comparison information and well-organized links. Where appropriate, it's a great idea to also give women the choice of how much time they want to spend and how they want to use the technology (by providing a text option alongside an audio or a video download, for example).

□ *Integrate your retail experience.* Cater to how workingwomen are likely to shop, and through which channels. For example, in-depth information serves a great purpose online, where women are likely doing more intense research. However, that extra detail may clutter a catalog or an in-store product description. On the returns front, demonstrate your understanding of women's busy lives by offering several options; for example, in-store returns of online purchases are a welcomed option provided by the typical retailers in most malls across the country.

□ *Fully utilize online channels.* As we mentioned above, the efficiency of the Internet realm is a direct match for a businesswoman's strategic buying mind. Fine-tuning your online efforts will not only keep your existing online customers happy, but it will also help forge great beginnings with any women who have been more tentative about online buying and are just now beginning to shop on the Internet.

WORKINGWOMEN-FOCUSED INDUSTRY STUDY: BUSINESS TRAVEL AND HOSPITALITY

Female business travelers are one of the fastest growing travel segments in the country. From better security to healthier room-service offerings and attractive health club facilities, this is certainly one of those cases where improving the product by focusing on women's needs helps better serve men as well. More and more hotel chains, from the W Hotels to Wyndham Hotels & Resorts and Hilton, have wisely changed design and layout and have further developed amenities to better serve their female customers, who now make up almost half of the business traveling public.[9]

Security is the first concern of women, with location and proximity to clients of secondary concern. Once they feel comfortable with a certain chain, female business travelers tend to stick with it. So, what are the women-specific changes that positively affect their choices?

Security, comfort and room amenities are key. As of late 2001, after a ten-year lull in hotel development, chains were actively marketing the design of new properties to women by including brighter lobbies, tighter security and more open spaces, all of which discourage the intrusion of strangers. A few specifics of the changes that have been made to accommodate women business travelers include:

▫ *Security.* In addition to having deadbolts on their hotel room doors, women want to be notified by phone before room service staff members knock on their door. With the woman traveler in mind, the W Hotels chain has developed more airy and open guestroom hallways, with a window at both ends, while other chains have been investing in more security cameras.

▫ *Food service.* Solo diners in heavily business-traveled hotels are no longer relegated to back corners of the hotel's restaurant. According to studies, many businesswomen actually prefer to eat in their rooms, so room layouts are now more likely to accommodate meal trays, while healthier, more nutritious cuisine is included on the room service menu.[10]

▫ *Design*. Hotels are being designed with a much more residential feel, eschewing dark and paneled decors. W Hotels, in particular, hosts a "living room" rather than a lobby, with plenty of spaces for a single traveler to feel comfortable. Wyndham Hotels & Resorts, as part of their "Women on Their Way" efforts, also promotes their more open and well-lit lobbies.

▫ *Extras*. It is in this "extras" category where you can see strong evidence of women-specific hospitality developments. W Hotel amenities include all-natural fiber furnishings in guest rooms, with particular attention to high-quality linens; special bathroom lighting and large bath areas; and in-room massage. Wyndham offers Herman Miller ergonomic work chairs and Premium pillow-top mattresses and bed linens in some rooms, with in-room Internet access, which is becoming standard in most business travel hotels. Many hotel chains, in an effort to really deliver for women, offer amenities like the Loews Vanderbilt Plaza Hotel's "do not forget" closet that includes everything from hosiery to neckties; or they provide a "technology butler" for those with computer-related questions. And, many of the large hotel chains, including the W, currently promote their pet friendliness (with some restrictions). That is an extra we can relate to!

Moms

Having children profoundly affects any woman's lifestyle and attitudes, so the "mom factor" can prompt big changes in a female consumer's shopping habits. Interestingly, it is her parenting style more than the ages of her children or traditional demographics that segment one mom from another.

Even before you add in that immeasurable emotional aspect of parenting (as in the huge new importance that child-proofed packaging takes on), moms represent a complex segment of women to reach with your marketing messages: They rarely sit in front of the television; the preferences of their kids may win out over their own; and they may be too distracted to care whether the shampoo they pick up is their usual brand.

But, there are a few ways to group moms that should help you develop your approach to them, whether you are selling food, cars, vacations, insurance, retirement plans, children's clothing or toys . . . did we leave anything out?

MOMS' MONEY

According to the U.S. Department of Agriculture (the agency that tracks family expenditures), an average-income family will spend $165,630 on a child by the time the child reaches eighteen.[11]

Parents with incomes of $38,000 to $64,000 spend $18,510 on miscellaneous items for the average child from birth through the age of eighteen. This includes spending on entertainment, reading material, VCRs, summer camps and lessons.[12]

Females outnumber males in the United States by about 5 million (nearly 4 percent more) and a significant percent have at least one child.[13]

Even if money were not a consideration, 48 percent of moms would choose to work part-time or full-time. Thirty-one percent would choose to work at home caring for their family, and 20 percent would select volunteer work.[14]

moms and advertising[15]

WHAT MOMS WANT IN ADVERTISING

Visible benefits to using the product

Pictures of cute kids

Solutions to everyday challenges

Ways to enrich their children

Safety information

Useful ideas or advice

Value

MOM'S FAVORITE ADS

Dodge Caravan: "What Idiot came up with 'stay-at-home moms'"

K-Mart: "Stuff of Life"

AT&T: "Working mom staying connected at the beach"

Hallmark: Varied ad campaigns

Disney: "Creating memories"

Sizzle and Stir: Dr. Ruth and Mr. T

Oxygen: "Miss America"

State Farm: Working mothers

MasterCard: "Priceless"

SunnyDelight: SunnyD

MOMS' BUYING FILTERS

How women define their own roles is the best way to determine both their category within the moms segment and what may influence their perspective of your brand. As we already know from our look at the various generational profiles, women really don't use their ages to define themselves. So, instead, we have to zero in on the more lifestyle-oriented factors to get to know the viewpoint of moms, in general.

Below are two mothering styles that should generally include most moms:

Tradition reigns. These mothers operate under fairly traditional gender roles. They stay at home with the kids while the father works. Some of these moms may be living a transitional version of this lifestyle, balancing the traditions of their own childhood with the more modern need for a woman to be out of the house making a living.

Innovation rules. Then, there are the less tradition-bound moms. Some of these innovative women may not have planned their pregnancies, remained unmarried or headed toward divorce. They may not have chosen it, but many are raising their children without the father's involvement. The ultramodern mother may also be innovative, rearing her kids in active partnership with the father, while working outside the home and pursuing other self-fulfilling activities.

As more women approach motherhood from a less traditional perspective, they will represent one of the biggest opportunities for marketers. By validating the women who are already going about motherhood in unconventional ways, and equipping struggling moms with the means to enhance their self-image outside of their day-to-day roles, marketers will reflect these women's concerns and succeed in building a solid long-term relationship with them.

REFLECTING MOMS IN YOUR BRAND

Given the gamut of mothering styles and purchasing habits, the following general tips will help you see your brand the way moms do. A few resonant ways to serve moms include:

Market to multitaskers. With time pressures an issue for all women, for moms especially, marketing approaches should be developed and delivered in ways that lend themselves to being received while women are engaged in other tasks. When was the last time you saw a mom quietly reading a magazine or focusing on a television show? Brands have to come up with ways to reach moms while they are doing the laundry, giving the kids a bath, feeding the dog or running errands.

For example, a financial services company found that, although many women with children wanted to increase their financial intelligence, seminars were too much of a hassle (arranging for baby sitters, for one). However, a series of focus groups revealed that e-mail courses followed by a free coaching session by phone were a good fit with moms' schedules.

Provide information over emotion. Savvy, information-gathering women, moms or not, will likely choose to utilize the Internet as a resource over television ads, as it will allow them the time to read or refer to later in their buying research. With their children's health and best interests top of mind, women simply can't afford to make the emotion-based purchasing decisions that are more the point of quick-hit radio or television spots.

Packaged-goods and pharmaceutical Web sites, for example, have become extremely important to mothers in their "Dr. Mom" roles. These sites tune into their practical concerns and provide nutritional and weight information; self-diagnosing tools for illnesses and injuries; and the ability to find correct dosages and possible side effects of medications.

Support their practical priorities. What matters to moms day-to-day is how to be most effective in their roles. Gourmet recipes or details on how to scrub the bathroom floor to perfection are not important; of more concern are practical solutions for helping her child learn to love reading or to build his or her confidence.

Address their sense of balance and perspective. Advertisers have taken the picture of the frantic, task-crazed mothers to an extreme, and, although it may be true to a degree, it is rarely inspiring. In reality, most moms lead a more organic and integrated life and are proud of how much they are able to get done in a day. A better marketing approach might be to present, with humor and admiration, the clever ways moms devise to make their lives work while averting potential disasters.

Marketing messages that speak to that sense of balance, perspective and innovation will resonate and be a refreshing change from the usual detergent and toy ads.

Educate them online. Moms, who will continue to be significant purchasers and purchase influencers in the future, are knowledge-hungry and continually educating themselves. After all, they've got to keep up with all the changes as their kids grow. For new moms especially, the wealth of online information and shopping options are proving to be an extremely convenient resource.

literature-loving moms unite[16]

Before launching *Brain, Child* magazine, Stephanie Wilkinson and Jennifer Niesslein did due diligence on their competition and their likely readership. From what they'd learned through their research, they chose to focus on a broad-based readership: moms who were likely in the age range of 25 to 50, and were, like themselves, underserved by the other available parenting and mothering magazines. From letters to the editor and other feedback, in addition to very basic readership surveys, they soon were able to more narrowly define their core audience:

Moms in the mid-30s to mid-40s age range

Moms with much more affluent household incomes than expected

Seventy-four percent have household incomes over $65,000

One third of readership is at-home moms

Eighteen percent work part-time from home, and only 5 percent work full-time

Their surveys didn't cover the education level question, but they did find out what other publications were read by those polled, which included: *The New Yorker, Parents, Mothering, Salon.com, Martha Stewart: Living* and *Utne Reader.*

NO CUPCAKE RECIPES HERE

In addition to finding out that their readers were simply passionate about reading, Stephanie and Jennifer also realized that *Brain, Child* was hitting a nerve for first-time mothers even more than for more experienced moms with several children. Any first-time parent is looking for information wherever she can find it, but *Brain, Child* readers were also enjoying reading about, and connecting with, experiences they'd shared in the voices of other mothers (sometimes quite famous authors, and other times not so famous writers). Reading about other women who were struggling emotionally with the weaning of their child, or who had found their new-baby's existence created a different and confusing dynamic with their husbands, was the connection they sought.

In addition, readers seem to connect with the humor and authenticity within the pages of each issue of *Brain, Child.* The humor is in reading about other moms whose only moment of solitude is escaping for two minutes to the bathroom, for example. And, while authenticity is part of their overall mission, it seems extra evident in the regular *Brain, Child* debate section. In it, actual mothers (and not famous-named doctors) write on topics like disciplining other people's kids or whether raising a pet is really an educational experience or another chore for mom.

MOMS-FOCUSED INDUSTRY STUDY: INFANT DEVELOPMENT

Finding companies that support them in their mom role can be especially important for women who are experiencing motherhood for the first time. Not only do they have to keep track of diapers, feedings and washing loads while just being there for their child, they'll also feel guilty if they don't do everything they can to enrich and nurture their infant's learning.

In recent years, magazines like *Brain, Child* (see the sidebar) and many other clothing and baby equipment retailers have heeded this call and made their content, Web sites and retail stores much more responsive and relevant to the fears and concerns of first-time moms. A great industry example is The Baby Einstein Company, created by a mom to market products designed specifically for infants and toddlers.

An award-winning creator of the infant developmental media, including videos, DVDs, discovery cards, books and audio CDs, Baby Einstein focuses on exposing babies to the amazing world around them. The company supports new moms by providing fun and stimulating ways for parents and caregivers to interact and enrich their children's lives—through the use of real world objects, music, art, language, science, poetry and nature.

What Baby Einstein provides speaks to the concerns and guilt of moms for a variety of reasons, which include:

Positive development for the child = guilt-free minutes off for mom. With a tagline like "Babies love us. Parents trust us," moms are sure to consider Baby Einstein products. The videos seem amateurish to adult eyes, but it takes about a minute of viewing beside an infant or a toddler to see that the simple but creative presentation entrances children. And testimonials on their site (Babyeinstein.com) tell stories about moms' appreciation of Baby Einstein videos in their children's lives. With words like "transfixed" and "mesmerized" used to describe the way infants and toddlers watch videos that teach them the alphabet and about animals and classical composers, how could you go wrong?

I love to hide around the corner and watch her react to the changing scenes on the television screen—I can always tell when her favorite part is next—she starts bouncing like mad!! Also, thanks to you, I get to take a shower every day, knowing that she is in good company.

—Mother's testimonial on Babyeinstein.com

Growing with moms' needs makes it easy for her. Tapping into the needs of new moms meant that this new infant development industry could only grow to serve moms further with toddler and child development products. Now owned by the Walt Disney Company, Baby Einstein has extended its line into dozens of books, flash cards and new videos. Then came the "juvenile products" line, with Baby Einstein rattles, teethers, bouncers, and other baby items as well as infant and preschool and plush toys. By growing along with their customers, Baby Einstein has clearly been inspired to push further brand development.

As kids grow to influence purchases, the brand is ready. As toddlers become preschoolers they are likely to hold some sway over their mother's purchases, and Baby Einstein is ready for that transition. The company has created some distance from the "baby" moniker with a new Little Einstein subbrand TV series that launches worldwide in 2004. The usual music, art, language, science, poetry and nature themes will be explored, but in a way that is more relevant to this slightly more independent group—so puppets will be missing from the mix.

Household Manager and Time-Challenged Shopper

A woman's view of your brand is based on the form and shape of her perspective on life, however that may have developed. Then, life doles out the filters (the generational characteristics, the life stages, the life transitions and roles) that will combine or interchange as she considers your products or services.

The roles of single woman, businesswoman and mom have been covered here, but we wanted to briefly touch on two other roles that affect how most women see your brand: as household manager and time-challenged shopper.

HOUSEHOLD MANAGER

When serving as household manager, a woman is all the more likely to take on the businesswoman traits she uses at work. In her home-management role, she will be researching major appliance purchases, overseeing subcontractors for a remodel, managing the family investments and scheduling the kids' play dates and sports activities, among other things like grocery shopping.

While tracking all of these "businessy" aspects of personal life, the Internet can be very helpful for a woman. Access to the Web, just as in her business role, will provide resources for making educated consumer decisions and saving major amounts of time. Furthermore, the Internet is a very safe realm in which to pose the "dumb" questions and study up on technical information for the woman who is continually educating herself to deliver the best choices for her family.

TIME-CHALLENGED SHOPPER

Despite their heavy load of responsibilities with kids, work and parents, women still handle 70 percent of all household duties. The challenge is finding time to get it all done, especially when many of the companies they need to contact operate on banker's hours. Brands can support women's time-challenged shopping by developing ways to come to them, such as: providing in-office massage, putting bank branches in grocery stores or offering on-site (her site) mobile car washes. If you help her to shop and get things done during her lunch hour and on breaks (for example, by staffing up your retail store from 11 a.m. to 2 p.m. on weekdays), you'll be part of a powerful trend that helps her cross things off her to-do list without compromising work hours.

Finally, the Internet has become a dream for time-challenged women who find they can indulge themselves in the "fun" of shopping or entertainment only at extreme off-hours late at night or very early in the morning. Their well-earned self-indulgent activities might include reading up on personal hobbies, visiting entertainment and celebrity Web sites or exploring interactive components of the Web. During these off-hours of shopping online, women may well view products and services through a more personal filter, and less through a household, task-focused one.

Understand Life Roles to Reach Women More Effectively

The more you understand life roles, the more your brand will reflect an awareness of how those circumstances affect a woman's days and her buying behavior. A woman could never be defined solely as a single woman, businesswoman or mom, but there is great insight to be gained by combining the cross-generational role factors with the common generational truths.

By examining the combination of life filters—generational, cross-generational life stages and roles, cultural influences—you develop an understanding of the incredibly unique women your brand serves. Studying all of these layers can only better prepare you to provide for the varied needs of the women's market for your products and services.

CHAPTER 7

cultural influencers
the buying filters of emerging majorities

THE HISPANIC, BLACK and Asian American market segments, until recently referred to as minority groups, are rapidly growing in numbers and economic influence.[1] In fact, we marketers had to drop the term "minority" altogether and call these segments what they really are: emerging majorities. The women of these emerging majorities are looking for brands that view them as a significant part of the future of the U.S. consumer market and already reflect the mix of their many cultures in the goods, services and marketing messages they deliver.

It may feel like the major growth among Hispanics, Blacks and Asian Americans has snuck up on us, but it really hasn't. The shrinking of the Anglo American majority seems to drive that point home. While Anglo Americans in 1990 represented 87 percent of the total consumer marketplace, by 2007 their market share is expected to decline to 80 percent of all U.S. consumer spending, and this downward trend will continue.[2]

Correctly using the many possible terms to describe these segments, like African American or Caribbean American or Hispanic American or Mexican American, is just the tip of the iceberg in training your brain to understand the women of these groups. We'll start by pointing out the common traits that are generally shared by these diverse cultures and that differentiate them from Anglo culture as a whole. Then, we'll go into a few more specifics on each of these three ethnicities to help define who these women are and what influences their buying decisions.

The Buying Filters of Emerging Majority Women

Whether your market is Hispanic, Black or Asian American women, an "in-culture" marketing approach should be the ultimate goal:[3] The keys to reaching them should reflect their truths as ethnic women, as well as honor the beliefs, traditions and values that differentiate them from women in the general marketplace.

There are a few overarching guidelines to consider when viewing your brand through the lens of an Hispanic, a Black or an Asian American woman:

Cultures and dialects vary even within each segment. Asian Americans, for example, have roots in countries with cultures and languages as diverse as those of India, Cambodia, and Japan.

Acculturation will vary, as well. Women who are first generation immigrants will likely hold much more strongly to the traditions of their homeland than will their daughters or granddaughters.

Religion is an important but sensitive topic. Special holy days and celebrations are very meaningful to members of these ethnic populations, but such strong faiths and traditions make it that much easier for marketers to offend (so be wary).

Family and domestic concerns remain important. Family gatherings are so traditionally ingrained with most of these segments that representing women from these ethnicities in an overly independent, more Anglocized way, might not resonate.

Clothing, hair and general appearance matter. A put-together and well-groomed look is yet another cultural standard for many women in these emerging majorities, which should be reflected in your marketing efforts. Interestingly, even though ethnic women seem more attentive to their appearance, the effects of aging may be less of an issue for them than for Caucasian women. As reported by the *Fort Worth Star Telegram*, "In general, African American, Hispanic, Asian and Native American women appear to be less worried about getting (and looking) older—partly because their skin is less quick to show signs of age, and partly because their cultural backgrounds offer them a different perspective."[4]

Language may still be a barrier. In response to acculturation levels, an effort should be made to communicate with people of Hispanic, Black or Asian American (or any other) ethnicity in their own language wherever possible. If nothing else, a bilingual approach in ads or promotions will be key for further demonstrating that your brand values its consumers' cultural heritage.

Certainly, you may be able to make an existing campaign more relevant to some of these emerging cultures with minor adjustments in tone. But usually, it will take more effort to craft messages and find images that resonate with the different cultures of these emerging majorities.

Honda, for example, has already realized the value of taking a multicultural approach. In mid-2002, the marketing savvy auto manufacturer launched three ad campaigns specifically targeted to

Hispanics, Asian Americans and Blacks. Their bilingual Hispanic TV effort, tagged "When was the last time a car sounded this good to you?" aired on Univision, Telemundo, VH1, Discovery and MTV. The Asian American spot was more celebration-oriented with a voice-over that said, "Introducing the all-new Accord. Let the celebration begin." And, the African American ad aired on UPN, WB and BET, featuring the tagline, "Redesigned Accord coupe from Honda. The attraction is obvious."[5]

Honda's well-done multicultural efforts should inspire us to learn more about marketing effectively to these emerging majorities. Let's take a quick look at some of the facts and marketing challenges specifically presented by the Hispanic, Asian American and Black women's markets to help you jump-start launching your own in-culture campaigns.

Hispanic American Women

The rapidly growing Hispanic population represents a huge marketing opportunity. According to the U.S. Census Bureau, between 1990 and 2000 the Hispanic population grew 58 percent, compared with Asians 48 percent and African Americans 16 percent.

With its buying power growing 12 percent annually, the Hispanic market is clearly one of the most influential consumer frontiers yet to be more fully tapped. Still, advertisers have only recently begun to include this group in their budgets.

National retailer Target is one brand that has both celebrated Hispanic culture and supported its youth. In 2002, Target (along with other big-name brands like Hewlett-Packard and Daimler-Chrysler) sponsored "Chicano," a pair of museum exhibits that will travel to fifteen cities over the course of five years. In addition to the exhibits, performances and other local events, three scholarships per city will be awarded to Hispanic youth.[6]

Although the Target-sponsored exhibits may be a good example of connecting with the Hispanic community, it remains a challenge to reach the women of this market, who may or may not be tuned into TV or the Internet. Let's see, then, what may be influencing Hispanic women's views of typical U.S. goods and services.

THE BUYING FILTERS OF HISPANIC AMERICAN WOMEN

Hispanic American women have emigrated from a number of different countries, each with its own culture and dialect. Further, acculturation levels vary depending on how long a woman has lived in the United States. What resonates with a woman of Cuban descent may need to be reworked to ring true with a woman of Mexican descent. And, first-generation Hispanic American women may hold tightly to their more family-oriented, hierarchical orientations, while their granddaughters may have already developed less ethnic lifestyles and self-images.

Using the term *Latina* or *Hispanic woman* depends on her preference and whether she considers herself more liberal (Latina) or more conservative (Hispanic). As it is too hard to guess about what your women consumers prefer, the best bet may be to use *Hispanic* when addressing them.

The younger generations of Hispanic American women add yet another wrinkle. M. Isabel Valdés has found that many of the culture's teens and young adults are also rediscovering their roots in both their language and traditions.[7] So, the lesson is to never assume we've "got it all down" when marketing to women, ethnic or Anglo, because the next generation may well blow our theories out of the water.

No matter what acculturation level or language preference, Hispanic women in general have family and household purchases on their minds. With families that often include grandparents, godparents and other relatives in addition to children, a typical Hispanic household's consumer decisions will likely be made by a broad range of women (including mothers, sisters and grandmothers). Furthermore, Hispanics are known to make shopping a family affair, with more than a third of those surveyed preferring to shop with their families.[8]

With the majority of Hispanic Americans holding Catholic beliefs, the many Catholic religious holidays, festivals and celebrations are of great importance within this culture and for entire extended families. Interestingly, Hispanic community loyalty may not necessarily translate into shopping preferences: Only 26 percent of Hispanics say they'd prefer to shop at a local store over a national chain.[9]

REFLECTING HISPANIC AMERICAN WOMEN IN YOUR BRAND

In our marketing efforts to reach Hispanic American women, how can we incorporate and reflect the significant cultural differences we've discussed? Language and acculturation levels, in particular, seem to be key.

In the case of the older population, AARP (formerly the American Association of Retired People) has found the two issues of language and acculturation to hugely differentiate Hispanic Americans from the general fifty-plus market.[10] Senior Hispanics may have limited or no knowledge of English, and they are more likely to live out their lives in multigenerational homes rather than in assisted-living residences.[11] For these elder Hispanics, it would seem to be more important to have Spanish-language in-person customer service connections, for example, than in-language ad campaigns.

Over time, all new Americans will certainly acculturate to some degree. But, wherever these women fall in the spectrum, from traditionally Hispanic to more Anglocized, it will be worth letting these influential consumers know that your brand understands them.

Above all, avoid generalizing about or stereotyping the Hispanic American market. The major cultural and dialectical distinctions within that vast population really can't be ignored in your marketing efforts.

That said, here are a few examples of ways to ensure that you present your brand clearly through a Hispanic woman's buying perspective:

Reflect acculturation differences. Older Hispanic women, or those still adhering to traditional roles, may not pursue work outside the home. So, images of women in business suits with cell phones will not reflect the realities of these women or speak to them. And, stay attuned to the ever-present language barrier: While some 51 percent of U.S. online Hispanics prefer to use English at home, 21 percent prefer Spanish and 27 percent use both languages.[12]

The launch of PepsiCo's Gamesa USA MiniPacks was a good example of in-culture marketing, reaching Hispanic mothers where they would normally be and through the media channels they regularly use. Launched in the summer of 2002, the campaign targeted Hispanic mothers with children under age 12, promoting MiniPacks' individually packaged cookies, in radio spots, subway car interior ads and newspaper rack headers for *La Raza*, Chicago's Spanish-language newspaper.[13] The tagline, "Perfectos Para Llenar el Hueguito" (Perfect to Fill the Hunger Gap), appealed indeed to the emotion-driven childrearing concerns of moms.

Show pulled-together fashion and make-up. While T-shirts, jeans and just lipgloss may resonate with most Anglo women, don't assume the same for Hispanic women. Their culture includes the tradition of family celebrations and, thus, they are likely comfortable dressing up a bit, and doing so more often.

Keep family and children in mind. A quarter of Hispanics say their kids have a significant impact on the brands they buy.[14] Furthermore, their typically larger families and greater hospitality concerns may also influence Hispanic women to purchase larger quantities of food and many packaged, ready-to-eat goods.

Tap into the local celebrations. As long as you have thoroughly done your homework and can respectfully participate or involve your brand in a religious or traditional celebration (via a sponsorship, for example), such events may be a great way to raise brand awareness among Hispanic women.

Be online and buy cable television time. There are about 12.4 million U.S. Hispanics accessing the Internet from home, work or a university.[15] And, that number will grow, as Richard L. Israel, comScore's vice president of Hispanic marketing solutions, recently noted: "Since Hispanic Web users tend to be younger and live in larger households, they are likely to be more comfortable with technology and exercise influence over their family members for purchases. And importantly, they can be efficiently reached through leading Web sites."[16]

As for television habits, a study of urban women conducted by Surveys Unlimited found that Hispanic, as well as Black, women are more likely than white non-Hispanic women to prefer cable television channels over traditional networks.[17] Furthermore, Black, Hispanic and Asian women in the same study expressed a greater interest than white urban women in the variety of features offered by digital television services.

Asian American Women

While Hispanic American women come from many different cultures, they share a somewhat common language. Asian American women, however, may not even have that trait in common. Having emigrated from countries as diverse as Japan, China, Korea, Indonesia, Pakistan and India, they are likely to communicate in a much wider variety of languages or dialects than their sisters from other emerging majorities. As marketers, we have to forget about reaching Asian American women en masse, but instead dial into the particular subsegment that best represents our customers.

Two elements of Asian cultures that have mattered for years and years, community and children, may be the keys to marketing to the women of this particular emerging majority. In fact, like many before them who came to our shores, "the leading reason for immigration cited by Asians is the desire to provide a better life for children."[18]

THE BUYING FILTERS OF ASIAN AMERICAN WOMEN

An Asian American woman's attitudes and buying behavior, and how these revolve around community and children, may reflect the social status and roles of women in their home cultures. For example, even when they work full-time, Asian American women continue to manage much of the household and overall family finances, just as they would in their home countries. Their cultures may lead them to do what they've always done (which is a lot) and to add in all the extras that are also expected of them in U.S. culture!

Many of the women in this often highly educated emerging majority will also apply the skills they've acquired from years of household management to become empowered to build their own businesses. Their education and business experience may actually make them a bit more progressive in comparison to Anglo American women or to those of other ethnicities with whom they affiliate. Meek, passive, geisha-type characters these women are not.

And, along with their education and business experience, these women have some major shopping skills. Asian consumers shop more than other groups, with almost half (43 percent) saying that they always look for a brand name when they shop.[19] But, interestingly, brand consciousness does not necessarily mean brand loyalty, with 25 percent of Asians saying they change brands often, as compared to 22 percent of Hispanics, 20 percent of Blacks and 17 percent of Anglos.[20] Furthermore, Asians are big Internet shoppers. While they are the least likely (compared with whites, Hispanics and Blacks) to buy merchandise by phone or mail order, they are the most likely to shop over the Internet.[21]

REFLECTING ASIAN AMERICAN WOMEN IN YOUR BRAND

As a rule of thumb, we highly recommend developing marketing messages that reflect the uniqueness of the many different backgrounds and cultures of Asian American women. Slapping a native language voice-over onto your existing television campaign would certainly not suffice.

Aegis Gardens retirement community, in contrast, could be considered a good example of delivering a more typical American experience in an in-culture way for aging Asian Americans. As described by Deborah Kong of the Associated Press: "With the assistance of the Chinese advisory board, the company changed its corporate color from blue, which Asians associate with funerals, to maroon, and petitioned the city's building department to change its street address because it contained the number 4, which is associated with death in Asian cultures."[22]

With the Aegis example in mind, the following tips should help you forge a better connection with the savvy and hard-working Asian American women who may be your customers:

Images of success resonate. In general, and in all but perhaps the Southeast Asian cultures, younger and older Asian American women alike are image-conscious. So, depict them in successful roles and don't forget the details of the appropriate outward appearance as well—the finest in clothing or jewelry, for example.

Learn and honor culturally specific traditions. Gift-giving occasions may be different for each Asian culture, and therein may lie significant opportunities to reflect your knowledge of the needs of these women and to serve them better.

Use the familiar to reach them. Just as women from the emerging majorities appreciate seeing their body types and skin colors represented in your marketing efforts, their cultural pride will be even greater when their native languages are used. Even as they become more acculturated, Asian American women still notice the companies that take the time and spend the budget to produce ads that quite literally speak to them and reflect their realities.

And, don't overlook the 1.5 generation. In the Asian American segment of the country's fast-growing multicultural population, the 1.5 generation is considered by Asia Link Consulting Group to be the "forgotten" generation that deserves attention. The 1.5 generation immigrated to the United States as children under age 18, brought by their parents who came by choice. The 1.5 generation straddles both the immigrant generation born outside the United States (usually called the first generation) and those who were born here, called the second, third and fourth generations.

the varied valentine's day gift-giving traditions of east asians[23]

In Japan, a country steeped in gift-giving tradition, Valentine's Day has been adapted as "Giri Choco," which means "obligatory chocolate," a primarily one-sided gift-giving tradition where females buy chocolate for their male counterparts. On this day, women buy chocolate for their boyfriends, husbands, male co-workers, classmates and their male superiors at work. When the men receive the chocolate gift, they are obligated to return the favor one month later, which is known as White Day. On White Day, unlike Giri Choco, the types of presents men give are more varied. They range from jewelry to candies and flowers.

The equivalent of White Day is also observed in Korea, where women give men chocolate on Valentine's Day and men give women candy a month later. Many Chinese follow the American tradition of Valentine's Day. However, the Chinese traditionally have their own version of Valentine's known as "Lover's Day," which falls on the 7th day of the 7th month in the lunar calendar. It is a celebration of a legendary love story involving a young mortal cow herder and an immortal weaving fairy. The Chinese believe these two lovers were separated by the Heavenly Mother and can only be reunited once a year, on the 7th day of the 7th month, when a bridge of birds will be formed in the sky. On this particular day, some Chinese still cherish this traditional festival and celebrate it with loved ones by buying flowers and other gifts.

The Japanese who adopted this Chinese myth celebrate the same holiday and call it "Tanabata-sama." In Japan, it is celebrated to this day with an annual street festival and involves the decorating of small bamboo trees with origami, where people write their wishes on oblong strips of rice paper and hang them on the trees.

Asian Americans are a very diverse ethnic group and they have different traditions and observe different holidays. It is important for marketers to understand and be sensitive to their individual customs and traditions when planning promotions and ad campaigns targeted to each group.

Black Women

Do U.S. companies adequately address the concerns and market needs of Black Americans? This sensitive issue has been getting more media coverage in recent years. And, while there has been a noticeable increase in the number of Black actors and models represented in ad campaigns, this minority and emerging majority, which includes a broad range of dark-skinned ethnicities, may still feel underserved.

THE BUYING FILTERS OF BLACK WOMEN

Like all women, Black women rightfully expect to feel respected as consumers and to be invited to partake of your brand. In general, if you respect their community and church involvement, and reflect those values that they hold dear, the women of this segment will be more inclined to focus their buying on the products and services you present to them.

According to recent reporting by *Newsweek*, 35 percent of Black women go to college as compared to 25 percent of Black men.[24] Furthermore, "College educated Black women already earn more than the median for all Black working men—or, for that matter, for all women."[25] This seems to set the stage for much of their consuming behavior—Black women are educated, they make the money and they manage the household.

Household management and family purchasing decisions, from groceries to automobiles, are more often made by Black women, as opposed to Black men, than is the case for the general marketplace. In 2002, the Fannie Mae Foundation found that more than two-thirds of African American women (68 percent)—compared to 55 percent of women overall—said that they were the only one who handled the household financial planning and budgeting. Furthermore, African American women tend to have more financial responsibilities because they are less likely than women overall to be married.

According to the 2000 U.S. Census, 47 percent of Black women in the thirty- to thirty-four-year-old age range have never married, compared with 10 percent of white women. Yet, these single Black women are adopting children in record numbers. The U.S. Department of Health and Human Services found that 32 percent of children who were permanently adopted through public adoptions in 2001 were adopted by single women, with over half (55 percent) of them Black women.[26]

Overall, there is great diversity of experience and expectation among Black women, depending on country of origin—whether African or Caribbean—and life experiences. Some experienced the changes of the Civil Rights era, while others did not live through that powerful time of transition. The level of a Black woman's sense of entitlement, which could greatly affect how she goes about making consumer purchases, might well depend on whether her experiences include years living under segregation or in a socially diverse environment.

Finally, of the three groups of women we've profiled in this chapter, Black women may be the most conscious of style. In fact, 34 percent of Black consumers say they like to keep up with fashions and trends, as compared to 28 percent of Asians, 27 percent of Hispanics and 25 percent of whites.[27]

REFLECTING BLACK WOMEN IN YOUR BRAND

Keeping the tone of a marketing message respectful and positive is a good place to start with any group of women, of course, but it's especially true in the case of Black women. As with the other emerging majorities we've covered, marketers should do their subsegmenting homework to reflect the key lifestyle factors of their customers in their promotions and messages.

A few more guidelines for developing messages that reflect an understanding of women within the Black population include:

Demonstrate your commitment to their communities. Sponsoring a neighborhood event is an effective grassroots method for connecting with Black women. Use local media channels (billboard ads, for example) as a powerful way to forge connections with these women. Furthermore, Black women often consider the churches they attend their true community centers.

As reported by *DiversityInc* magazine in late 2001, "Church, for many African Americans, is far more than a place of worship. The church may double as a health center, school, bookshop, counseling center, job-placement center, early childhood development center and more."[28] Though some marketers may try hawking all sorts of goods at African American churches, business should never interfere with their spiritual and religious purposes.

Value their lifestyles and cultural diversity. While older Black women may have lower expectations for inclusiveness in ad campaigns, their daughters or granddaughters are more likely to expect marketing messages that reflect their experiences with racial and cultural diversity. They also expect to be included or represented in ad campaigns as the businesswomen, students, athletes and mothers that they are.

Tap into their popular cultural interests. The music and fashions of Black teens have been hugely influential in the early twenty-first century, and Black female musicians, in particular, are much more visible (and successful) than in years past. Using these cues and tapping into Black popular culture within your marketing messages will reflect your brand's to-the-minute knowledge of their interests.

Reflect their use of media channels. The community focus of a Black woman's life is visible in the pages, on the sites or in the broadcasts of the variety of culture-specific media channels she uses. Interestingly, however, their culturally specific newspapers seem to be losing the battle for attention with this emerging majority, just as newspapers are losing ground with the general public. The media channels most often used by Blacks now include mainstream media in addition to Black-oriented magazines, radio stations, television programs and Web sites.[29]

In-Culture Marketing Keeps Your Brand in Focus

Because the consuming ways of Anglo American women have just recently come into sharper focus for many marketers, we may too easily default to marketing to them when developing a new campaign.

But, the facts are in: Hispanic, Asian and Black Americans are the three key markets poised for major expansion in the United States during the coming years.

Knowing what we do about how much women, in general, influence consumer spending, it behooves us as marketers to focus in on what makes the women of these ethnic groups see our brands clearly and positively. Our marketing efforts should become in-culture in step with a marketplace that now has an increasing number of skin colors and cultures.

There is so much to learn about female consumers in the emerging majorities that you can't just dip your toe in the water. Rather, you've got to dive in and fully commit to continuing your education in how to reach them. Do whatever you can to discover what cultural cues might be influencing their view of your product or brand.

When they see your brand reflecting their culture and community—through event sponsorships, in-language billboards or ethnically specific offerings (such as food products)—that's when the women of these hugely influential markets will stand up and take note of what your are doing. And, that's how they will all get the best perspective of what your product or service has to offer them.

CHAPTER 8

learning curves and life stages
relationship-building opportunities

CONVENTIONAL WISDOM often prompts marketers to target young people because brand preferences are established early in life. Although some brand preferences are established in youth, there are other windows of "brand openness" in customers' lives when companies have a lucrative opportunity to capture the attention of first-time buyers and shift dollars away from the competition.

When a customer faces a steep learning curve prior to a purchase (such as buying stocks or mutual funds) or experiences a life transition (such as having a baby), a significant number of new brand decisions are made. Because such customers need extra support during these times, they represent prime opportunities for building strong customer relationships and cultivating deep brand loyalty. And the best news for marketers is that these learning curves and life transitions occur multiple times throughout a person's life, not just when customers are young.

In this chapter we will explore the role confidence plays in the buying cycle and then take a closer look at the life transitions that women navigate throughout their lives. With customers hungry for tailored information and customized support, you will learn how your brand can be in the right place, at the right time, delivering the precise information customers are seeking.

The Confidence Question: How Education and Experience Filter a Woman's Buying Mind

As marketers we have to be prepared for the wide range of comfort levels about different industries that might filter the buying minds of women. For example, purchasing toothpaste may seem easy, but what about the buyer's confidence in purchasing baby equipment (when there is so much new emotion attached) or in knowing how to buy life insurance? There is a danger of alienating more tentative buyers by not providing foundational information necessary to make a purchase, especially for the first time. On the other end of the spectrum, those companies that take a more elementary approach to their markets may find that more confident consumers skip over their brands, feeling their sales people, products or services are not sophisticated enough.

This lack of understanding about how to address both tentative and confident customers has elevated those companies that do get it right above the crowd and positioned them for success.

Because people can vary so widely in the knowledge and experience they bring to the table, it is important to explore the ways to address them wherever they are in the learning and buying process. For industries that traditionally require a high learning curve—like financial services, home improvement, electronics or even something that should sound fun, like snowboarding—the fear of the unknown may be the greatest barrier to drawing in a woman as a customer.

To best prepare for all confidence levels, you should provide a variety of entry points to your sales process and keep the learning environment comfortable and supportive. In the end, the newly empowered female customer you've shepherded through to a purchase will likely have become your biggest fan and most passionate evangelist.

Provide for a Range of Confidence Levels

If your market research zeros in on the data, averaging out the numbers for your core female customers, you might miss the vast differences in your consumers' confidence levels. Be careful that you identify and develop a plan for serving all groups of customers on your industry-confidence spectrum. One group of your prospective female customers, for example, might be fluent in your industry's language and comfortable with the transactions involved; while another group might be just beginning to grasp the basics and feel a bit intimidated.

If you skew toward serving those at the confident end of the spectrum, you won't resonate with your tentative consumers. And, if you skew toward the tentative customers, you'll frustrate those who are much more familiar with your industry and know exactly what they want to do and how they want to purchase your product. Sounds like you can't win for losing, but never fear.

The best way to honor any particular customer's time and knowledge is to customize your delivery at several levels. When you do this, you can both carefully draw industry newcomers through the process, and still provide advanced materials and offers that your more industry-familiar women can utilize and benefit from.

If yours is an industry to which some groups of women will be new customers, you might plan to develop several confidence-building "touch points" to better serve them along the way. This might mean something as basic as the option of speaking with a human being, twenty-four hours a day if need be, to help them use the technology of your online store; or it might mean doing a follow-up phone call after an in-person meeting at your bank to make sure all of her questions about your product were fully answered. By incorporating human interaction and communication between your employees and your customers into the daily mix of your business, you can more easily take the pulse of your targeted market subsegments, while monitoring your customers' learning processes as a whole. Then, you can be more responsive to your customers' changing needs and expectations, regularly tweaking your sales and marketing process in real time.

No matter what, women of all confidence levels will appreciate the options you provide to help them learn more about your product or industry, or so they can just shop with ease on your Web site.

Guidelines for High Learning Curves

The products or services with high learning curves should be pretty easy to recognize, because they require a significant amount of information to consider prior to making a purchase. Yet, there are some industries that may seem as though they'd be hard to learn at first glance, but because they've been in the consumer business for so long, the buying process involved has become second nature to most customers.

Making decisions about your investments for your children's college years may have a high learning curve, for example. But buying deodorant should be fairly simple (but it may have been an odd thing for consumers to think about way back when it first became available). And, buying a new water heater may involve some depth of self-education for the female consumer, while most adult women have likely long since studied up on how to buy a car. It just varies from industry to industry.

TENTATIVE TESTERS

Whether a woman approaches your brand as a first-time buyer in your category or as an experienced purchasing agent, she will be looking for different needs to be met. On the front end of that spectrum is someone who may be more tentative in her exploration.

A tentative tester's process may begin with outreach to friends— "Have you purchased a lawn mower before? What do I need to think about?"—and then turn to Internet research. The information-gathering woman may then return to pose questions to her friends from a more educated angle, as in: "I'm weighing the electric versus gas-powered mower question from the environmental angle. What have you found?" Once she's gathered that much information, she'll likely head back to the Internet to compare features, benefits, prices and retail outlets.

If your brand has stayed in touch with customers all along, it should be on the tentative woman's radar right from the start of her prepurchase process. For example, the friends of a "newbie" may have long since been purchasing your brand, or your brand may have developed a reputation for using conversational (not industry lingo) search keywords on its retail site. (After all, "apparel" isn't the first thing on our minds when we hit our favorite online shops, but "clothes" certainly are.) Your site should present easy-entry learning options for a new consumer, long before she ever approaches the finality of a shopping cart. Remember, there is a difference between making something *simple* and making it *clear.* Tentative customers new to your industry may not necessarily need material dumbed-down for them.

If a woman's friends aren't already suggesting your brand during her first round of exploration, you do need to ensure that it comes into a woman's view at the Internet and search engine stage.

Study the natural progression in the decision making of your tentative, testing, soon-to-be-purchasing female consumers and use that knowledge to be right where you need to be when they are ready for it. Is your brand listed very close to the top of search engine results when a woman types in your product name or type? For example, is your brand of natural estrogen a name that is top of mind for a woman's naturopath, so it will get mentioned during the course of her decision making about a menopause supplement? Accessibility to your brand (is your URL easy to recall?) and perfect timing (when her first child was born did your bank send information about starting a college fund?) will be the jump start for furthering your brand's awareness among women.

CONFIDENT CONSUMERS

On the other end of the tentative-confident spectrum are those who are likely to have been early adopters of your technology, or for some other reason just dove right in to your high-learning-curve industry. If you assume the lowest common denominator for these savvy buyers, the ways you deliver your product or service may be too agonizingly slow or time consuming for their quick thinking and acting. So, in the same way you deliver more thorough options for tentative consumers, you should present your more confident consumers with HOV lanes to guide them speedily through their buying processes.

Confident women consumers will be further along in their education process. They will already have spoken with friends, done the research, spoken with friends again, read comparisons and possibly interviewed or tested a few of your competitors. They have already accumulated the learning or the tools to make the decision and are looking for the company that will most resonate with them and efficiently serve them.

So, while it should be easier to serve them, it will also be more likely that you'll frustrate these confident shoppers. For example, there's nothing like a long form to complete prior to using the shopping cart to make a savvy customer lose patience and head to your competition.

Our advice is to ease their way. Remove the speed bumps and widen the access roads for this group of confident women. They are ready to be strategic and efficient about their purchase. The natural progression along their decision-making path needs to be served, just as with the tentative group, but in this case your brand needs to provide ways to skip over the basics. For example, by offering a "quick buy" link on your site for regular shoppers who've long since given you their profile information, you've catered to those technology- and Internet-confident customers (and we thank you).

TIPS TO REACH BOTH ENDS OF THE CONFIDENCE SPECTRUM

The following tips will help you focus your marketing messages and product information on both tentative and confident buyers, with easy entry points for all:

Ask her where she is in the process. Train your sales and customer service staff to ask female customers where they are in their buying processes; and, then respond accordingly.

If a woman says she is just looking, your staff should find out what information she needs and provide it by e-mail or, if she prefers, a phone call later in the day. If a woman says she is ready to buy, your staff should trust that she is (and not pester her with further questions) and make the transaction ultrasmooth and efficient from that point on.

Provide a range of education. Offer a selection of educational materials to help customers progress through the basic information stage and onto more advanced topics.

Teach related skills. Offer resources (online worksheets, seminars, brochures and one-on-one instruction) that will educate interested consumers about your industry and on making wise purchases within it. Be the source for the insider secrets and information that develop a tentative shopper into a more sophisticated consumer. For example, a nursery could offer topical classes for both "New Gardeners" and "Master Gardeners."

Map key information points. Consider what key information customers need prior to making a purchase decision. Explore how your educational materials, sales presentations and other resources support this natural learning and deciding progression.

Expand online options. Web sites, e-mail campaigns and other online tools should be fully developed to accommodate and equip both industry-tentative and industry-confident women. For example, a Web site can provide low-tech (phone) and high-tech (real-time chat) online customer service options to serve women at both ends of the technology spectrum. For e-mail, tending to low and high confidence levels might mean something as simple as making sure you deliver text e-mail messages as well as HTML.

how tentative prospects become confident buyers: marketing truths emerge from a snowboarding clinic[1]

One of us (Andrea) interviewed Yvonne Kidd, editor and publisher of the very inspiring site, Skilikeawoman.com, and Sue Greene, ski instructor and women's program head at Keystone Resort, to learn from their years of experience in the snow sport industry. Their thoughts, along with my interpretation (in parentheses) of how they might be applied to other industries, are as follows:

□ When women become moms, their fear factor increases because they can't afford to get hurt, and, in general, they fall off the snow sport radar when they hit their "family formation" years. (How do the "mom" emotions change and affect women's perception of your product or service? How do you attract them again, once their kids get a little older?)

▫ Females clearly need different teaching techniques than men. Keystone's research found that "gaining confidence and reducing fear" and "improving style" were important reasons for women to take lessons. (How women want to learn about your products or services may differ greatly from the way men would go about it, too).

▫ There are a lot more single-parent households these days and snow sports are too expensive for them. (How can your product or service keep from being dropped off the "to-buy" list when a household's financial situation changes?)

▫ Women trust role models and instructors with whom they can identify and relate. Women will be more likely to trust a female ski instructor who has learned to master the mogul fields than a young male coach, for example. (Women need to be able to identify themselves within your marketing efforts and customer experience, or they'll think less of your brand for its lack of understanding.)

▫ Encourage women in your industry to serve as teachers, role models, presenters, key customer service representatives and the like. (Just as female snow sport customers appreciate female instructors, so will your women's market notice whether your management, advisory board, sales and customer service staff reflect female involvement, and, it may well affect their purchasing behavior.)

The best way to feed these varying confidence or comfort levels within your consumer markets is to provide options that most any customer could utilize. As we have seen, that might mean customizing your delivery at several levels to draw newcomers through the process carefully, all the while honoring the savvy customer's time and knowledge with quick information and purchasing tools. Some companies do this by offering a free membership that will automatically deliver the customer to an advanced area of the site, thus skipping any of the introductory information.

However, you've got to remember that your women's market is constantly evolving and learning, so don't figure that once you've done one study of their confidence levels you can call it quits. It will be important to check in regularly to see how your customers have progressed and then redevelop your approach and the technology that serves them.

If you keep the prepurchase learning environment comfortable and supportive of all levels of industry confidence, your female customers will remember, spread the word among their friends and be converted into regular customers.

The reward is that most women, once they've learned the basics of any new industry and have had their interests piqued, will speed to a full and sophisticated understanding of the topic. And, those women make great customers!

Life Transitions: An Open Door for New Brand Relationships

It is during life transitions, or those life phases of significant change, that brand relationship-building opportunities truly abound and a great number of brand decisions are made. Focusing on life stages is definitely not a new idea; in fact, many people can recall their passage into adulthood being marked by a sudden deluge of credit card applications in their college dorm mailboxes. New homeowners have also been in the focus for marketers. For years new additions to a neighborhood have been greeted by the "Welcome Wagon," which has progressed over time from a neighborly visit over pie to a mailbox loaded with offers from companies like Home Depot and the local fitness center. Recently, marketers have begun to give life-stage marketing more attention, especially in marketing to women, and are becoming more sophisticated in how they use transition periods to attract new customers.

Life transitions are important for marketers because they are moments of brand reflection, brand consideration and brand decision. A transition requires a more conscious decision-making process and may result in customers exploring alternative paths or displaying a greater openness to new ideas and options. During transitions people think not only about what they need (retail space for a new business venture, for example), but they may also reexamine how to best fulfill those needs. These seasons of change cause customers to revisit their standards on quality and value, such as purchasing hardwood floors for an office space instead of a lower-quality carpet. As they enter new life stages, customers often make upgrades, seriously considering new brands and checking out new industries for the first time.

COMMON LIFE TRANSITIONS FOR WOMEN

Encompassing both happy and sad experiences, the stressful and emotional times we call "transitions" actually happen quite regularly in the course of a typical person's lifespan. Sometimes, they even repeat themselves, in the case of marrying and divorcing, for example.

Because these transitions do happen fairly often, there is all the more reason for marketers to study up and become aware of these opportunities to appear within a woman's view. A few typical life transitions include:

Going away to college

Marriage or partnership vows

Birth or adoption of children

First house or apartment (away from parents)

Career or job change

Separation or divorce

Birth of grandchildren

Retirement

Death of significant other

Illness or death of parent

Sandwich generation responsibilities (simultaneously taking care of parents and children)

Empty nesting (all kids grown up and out of the home)

LIFE TRANSITION TRENDS

Not surprisingly, new trends in life transitions have developed at the same pace as our society and culture. Let's look at a few of these trends and how they might shape a marketing focus on women customers.

Women typically navigate through the change. Because women often make the buying decisions surrounding transitions, much of the emotional and physical burden rests on their shoulders. Whether newly seeking childcare, going through a divorce, experiencing empty-nest syndrome or caring for an elderly parent, women will deeply appreciate the extra service and support your products and services can offer them during stressful times.

Reruns are now common. Life transitions previously considered one-time events now commonly occur more than once. For example, marriage, raising a family and divorce sometimes reoccur at multiple times in a woman's life. It will be important for marketers to avoid a limited view of the typical age range for certain transitions and to cultivate customer satisfaction with your product or service, as many women will return to the same brands for assistance the second time around.

Timelines are shifting. The life transitions once traditionally associated with youth have shifted upward. Many women, for example, now experience their child-rearing years in their late thirties, forties or even fifties. Women are living longer and more youthful lives: But, when you think of those extra ten or so years, don't visualize them tacked onto the end of her life; instead extend her active forty- to sixty-year-old life stage to get a more accurate picture of her actual lifestyle.

"Mature" transitions are more frequent. Market opportunities for transitions of maturity are increasing. As Baby Boomers age, more women will be undergoing transitions like menopause, retirement, second marriages and grandparenthood. But marketers beware: This group of senior citizens will require you to reinvent your "senior" marketing ways to reinforce their youthful self-image.

HOW LIFE TRANSITIONS CAN INTERSECT WITH YOUR BRAND

A life transition can force a woman to zoom in on these concentrated decision-making times and lose her usual wide-angle perspective on life. When everything is going great, women certainly do appreciate good service and quality products, but when life gets more complicated, such service and quality will be all the more remembered.

For consumers experiencing a life transition, everything is new, including brand names, product categories and price ranges. Instead of taking advantage of the confusion to create a quick sale, brands that seek to partner with consumers through this accelerated education process will gain new business and deeper loyalty. Let's take a look at ways to partner with customers during life-stage transitions.

Help her get up to speed. She is often making multiple decisions in a concentrated amount of time so provide educational content including how things work, how they're used, what the options are and (maybe most important) what to do if things go wrong. In general, the Internet is the most logical channel for this type of information.

Tap into the human element. Whether the product is a high-tech gadget or low-tech clothing, an insurance policy or an automobile, women caught up in life transitions will always connect with the human side you present in their times of need. State Farm Insurance knows that their services often intersect with emotion-filled life transitions. In response, they highlight the ability to develop a long-term relationship with a local agent with slogans like, "We live where you live" and "Like a good neighbor, State Farm is there."

Create clarity through relevant associations. Life transitions often trigger first-time purchases. A key to introducing a consumer to a new product is building an association with a familiar concept. For example, a company that creates software for computer maintenance might describe their product as, "Spring cleaning for your hard drive."

Group products and information into sets. A woman preparing to paint her living room might find a basic "painter's starter kit" as a welcome time-saving solution, which includes a paint roller, a tray, a drop cloth, tape and smaller brushes. "Newlywed kits" are another good example of serving people during a stressful life transition or change point. According to *The Wall Street Journal*, county clerks are passing out plastic bags full of free samples and coupons for products to couples applying for marriage licenses.[2] Distributed by Time Warner's *Parenting Group* magazine, these kits include both their products and other company's products (for a fee). As so many people in Gen Y are reaching the prime time for marriage (their twenties), the number of packets given out will only increase in number. As the same article cited, research by Condé Nast indicates that couples buy more in the first six months of marriage than a settled household does in five years. Proof enough that the marriage life transition is a prime time to get your brand front and center.

Be a trusted filter. Build a network of solid companies and specific individuals that you refer to customers, and you will exponentially increase your value to the women you serve. For example, a legal firm that shepherds a just-widowed woman comfortably through getting her affairs in order, and personally links her with reliable and trusted people for her related needs, will be hugely rewarded by her trust and continued patronage.

Address multiple needs. Financial service companies are a good example of an industry that attempts to address a full spectrum of needs through a single company. A woman experiencing the transition of marriage might take advantage of a variety of services including: new checking and savings accounts, a change in investments (possibly including one for future children's college expenses), life insurance, retirement planning, prenuptial agreements, mortgages and home owner's insurance.

Internet-based metamarkets are taking the idea of addressing multiple needs to a new level. Metamarkets like Babycenter.com for mothers and Theknot.com for brides are consolidating and concentrating product education, comparison shopping and buying into a central location. The concept of metamarkets stems from a simple, yet profound, insight: Customers think about products and markets very differently from the way products and markets are actually bundled and sold. Customers think in terms of related activities, while companies tend to think in terms of products. Activities that are logically related in cognitive space may be spread across very diverse providers in the marketplace; yet they form a single market in the minds of customers. Their boundaries are derived from activities that are closely related in the minds of customers, and not from the fact that they are created or marketed by related firms in related industries, or even unrelated firms in unrelated industries.

Consider the activities associated with home ownership. From an activity perspective, customers view home buying, home financing, home maintenance, home repair and home improvement as all logically related. This activity cluster can be viewed as the "home ownership metamarket." In the marketplace, however, homeowners must deal with real estate agents, banks, mortgage firms, newspapers, plumbers, electricians, lawn care services, maid services, home improvement stores, home remodeling contractors, architects and interior designers to perform this set of activities and to satisfy this set of related needs. In doing so, customers must search, evaluate, and negotiate with a large number of service and product providers.

By easing the anxiety of life transitions, and being there right when a woman needs you, your brand will have made a great start in building a long-term customer relationship.

SERVE THE WIDER PICTURE SO SHE CAN ZOOM IN

Unfortunately, the stresses and challenges of these life transitions are never just an overnight problem. The duration of the change may be longer or shorter, depending on the woman and the situation. So, brands need to develop ways to provide real support to these women over time.

For example, adapting to a divorce or to a new household of children thanks to a new marriage or a melded family may involve challenges that endure much longer than anticipated. By delivering customized products and services along with specially trained staff to understand such life crossroads, brands will develop the ongoing supportive relationships that go beyond the surface and truly equip women as needs arise.

If the stress of the transition itself weren't enough, somehow women have to keep the rest of their lives functioning as well. They certainly can't neglect the many roles they play or the many plates they must keep spinning just because a major life crossroad has been reached!

As a woman goes through a career change, for example, her personal life won't suddenly stop moving around her. It's just not possible for her to focus in and do her transition processing in a vacuum without distractions from the rest of her life.

How can your brand provide support if its products or services aren't directly life-transition related? By easing the other tasks she may have, or the roles she may be playing (as mom, businesswoman, household manager), and giving her the room to breathe, you offer a woman a cushion.

So, even though your product or service may not be front and center for a woman during her life transitions, your brand may still be able to provide the ever-so-important buffer zone that gives her the headspace to tend to the transition.

the internet-
savvy woman

connecting with her online

SPEND A DAY with even a handful of American women and you'll see that going online has become a way of life for them—for gathering information, shopping and communicating with friends and family. So, to reach women where they are already assembling, you have to go online too.

Consumers are heading online in huge numbers. In fact, 10 million U.S. consumers were predicted to have gone onto the Internet during 2003, a growth of 6.5 percent over 2002.[1] To put that into perspective, in 2004 there are nearly two times as many online households as off-line households. What a difference a few years make!

More specifically, women comprise a slight majority of the total U.S. at-home Web population—52 percent female versus 48 percent male.[2] And, there's every indication that their numbers online will continue to increase rapidly.

Women are online for both community and shopping. In December 2002 alone, women's online communities, including sites like iVillage.com and Womensforum.com, reached approximately 30 percent of all female Internet users age 25 to 64, attracting a total of nearly 35 million visitors.[3] The segment of the online population that actually shops there, the majority of which is women, will grow 29 percent, from 93 million in 2002 to 121 million in 2005.[4] The amount online shoppers in general will spend at e-retail will skyrocket 93 percent, from $45.5 billion in 2002 to $88.1 billion in 2005.

How Do Women View and Use the Internet?

Though women make or influence the bulk of consumer purchases in the United States today, they no longer have much time to devote to traditional shopping, driving from store to store, so they are heading online. And, even given their initial privacy and security concerns, women seem to be rapidly gaining comfort shopping online.

To serve their preferences and to keep these savvy women lingering longer, Web sites will have to improve in functionality and customer experience. Web sites will also have to compete with the other media a woman is likely to be using simultaneously. In fact, and according to BIGresearch, a leader in online marketing intelligence, the Internet is the medium least likely to command the undivided attention of either working women or young moms—with 67 percent of women who go online regularly or occasionally doing so while also watching television.[5]

Giving women control online of how they receive information and interact with your company is hugely important to serving them well. When you address the bulk of their technology comfort anxiety right from the start, and guide them into more savvy use of your site (and the Internet in general), they can't help but love your brand.

By accommodating their range of Internet access (dial-up to broadband) and providing options other than downloading software, your awareness of the ways women deal with technology will be appreciated by your customers. If you give women a sense of control in their interactions with your site, they'll more likely remain loyal to your brand over time. And, once women know they've got some control, their view of the role the Internet plays in their lives becomes very positive.

The following are areas you can address to better reach both your high- and low-tech customers:

Connection speed. What percentage of your customers have broadband access? It might be worth having regular access to a computer without a high-speed connection to get a sense of how your site performs for this group. In addition, if most of your customers use AOL, make sure you have accommodated their different e-mail needs as well.

Software download alternatives. Since a significant group of your desired consumer base will not bother to view materials and demos that require software downloads, give them e-mail options or other ways to get the information they need from your company.

Samples and examples. Give them a glimpse of the big picture in advance, and many women will feel more comfortable entering into a new process or new brand relationship. For example, offer an initial sample e-mail from your e-mail training series or provide a step-by-step outline for participating in a Webinar (Web seminar), with testimonials from other women about how great and easy it was to do. An off-line example of this concept would be the way home improvement stores provide a floor display of a fully assembled kitchen or bathroom to provide a context and a visual example of utilizing the individual materials and products for sale. Then, when a woman comes into the store for a light fixture, for example, she'll more likely consider remodeling an entire bathroom, or at least feel inspired to buy a few more items for that room. (Displaying the big picture can be very effective indeed.)

Navigation control and viewing options. Provide both high- and low-tech options (watch streaming video or read text), as well as beginner and advanced paths through your process (read or skip introductions, view demos or go straight to checkout).

Human touch in customer service. Just because it can all be done on the Web does not mean that high-tech is the best choice for your customers. If women are more likely to be the buyers of your products, give them access to a human connection wherever possible. Just knowing it is there is a plus. Also, consider listing your brand's designated experts' e-mail addresses on your site in order to create the personal touch and stronger brand relationships for higher quality buying opportunities (instead of info@yourcompany.com, display NancyJones@yourcompany.com, even if "Nancy Jones" is your customer support group).

E-mail as the common denominator. If women customers are not taking advantage of your site's technology-driven bells and whistles, you should consider meeting their needs via e-mail. E-mail is a comfortable and valued tool for those women who are new to what the online world can do, especially as it helps with day-to-day communication with family and friends. It may be worth a test to see how much participation in a new program or seminar increases when you use e-mail instead of forcing software downloads or other technological extras.

INTERNET = TOOL, FRIEND AND ADVISOR

It's increasingly difficult, if not impossible, for most people to bank and shop during traditional retail hours. Even with so many information and entertainment media channels available, women seem drawn to simplicity and efficiency in their multiple-constituent and multiple-role lives.

In many ways, the Internet has become a timesaving appliance for women. They use the Web as a twenty-four-hour resource to streamline their information gathering and to stay in touch with friends who are in that same fully booked situation. In a 2002 study, late Baby Boomer and early Gen Y women, in particular, were more likely than men of all ages to agree that they are doing more shopping on the Internet than ever before.[6]

Most women begin their online experience by tapping into the "Internet as friend" by trying e-mail. Then, they quickly get up to speed and seamlessly incorporate e-mail and online research into their daily connections with family, friends, colleagues and businesses—making the Internet their tool and advisor, as well.

INTERNET = SHOPPING EFFICIENCIES

Off-line shopping can go from being a huge pain, running in and out of stores to buy household and family items, to being pleasurable for its social, "girlfriend fun" way. But, the Internet is quite a different realm for shopping. For many women, it's more about getting online, making the purchase and proceeding to the next task. Until technology advances beyond methods of sharing a page with a friend (which we're sure it will), the social aspects of shopping have not yet quite transitioned online.

In fact, women usually enter into the Internet buying process with a serious mission in mind. They've compiled their list (for example, shoes for Junior, wedding present for Sis, new speakers for the kitchen), done their research and now are strategically heading to the best site to make their purchases.

Developing intuitive e-commerce is a crucial part of making sure your site contributes to the efficiency of a woman's time shopping online. It's a matter of designing your site according to the way women think when making purchases in your industry. REI.com, for example, makes shopping easy, indeed, by organizing products by sport and in groupings like "Gear Checklist" and "How To Choose." The way the information and products are organized is so helpful, we go to the site just to help pack for a hiking trip whether or not we are buying gear. (Of course, we'd then likely buy anything we were missing from REI.com.)

Internet technology, combined with some study of how women buy and how to make the experience on your site intuitive, makes shopping online efficient and secure, in general. For that, all those women who squeeze shopping into the free corners of their day are thankful.

WOMEN AND MEN SWITCH SHOPPING BEHAVIORS ONLINE

Women utilizing the Internet as tool and advisor become ultraproficient online. They know just what they want and quickly make their purchases. This behavior seems like the opposite of their more social shopping behavior off-line, where roaming the aisles can be considered a carefree, relaxing pleasure or a social occasion with friends.

In contrast, men are more likely to meander and surf online, but they know exactly where to go in the mall to buy the thing they need and then run (and we mean run) out. This off-line shopping behavior may not apply when men are shopping at electronics or computer or gadget stores, however.

It is interesting to consider how men and women seem to switch their buying behaviors from off-line to online. Perhaps we can learn more from Envirosell president and founder Paco Underhill, who notes this difference between each gender's interest or use of off-line technology in his book, *Why We Buy: The Science of Shopping*: "Everywhere in the world of hardware and software, the sexes swap places: Men love to browse and wander while women are purposeful, impossible to distract while they look for what they need."[7]

For example, at a computer software store studied by Envirosell, the shoppers were mainly male, but the percentage of shoppers who actually made a purchase was highest among women. This fact seems to be the result of women being, as Underhill puts it, "in the store with some practical mission to carry out, not just to daydream over a new Zip drive or scanner. Most women would rather just learn what they need to know to use the damn thing."

Furthermore, according to Underhill, women "take technologies and turn them into appliances. They strip even the fanciest gizmo of all that is mysterious and jargony in order to determine its usefulness. Women look at technology and see its purpose, its reason— what it can do." For men, technology can often be viewed as more of a toy and a rich source of entertainment, which might explain the reversal in shopping behavior online.

As consumers, women demand more than men from the promise of a product or service, including the complete shopping experience surrounding the buy. Marketers need to face the fact that although women as a group are by no means easy to reach (we've never said they were), the Internet channel can likely provide the greatest access to their buying minds.

WOMEN'S ROLES ONLINE

As we discussed in Chapter 5, "Shaping the Generations," women lead multiple lives with overlapping, complex responsibilities and interests. These many factors shape their off-line buying behavior, but also hugely affect their reasons for going online and how they'll behave as e-consumers once there.

Research has shown that the best way to segment women online is by the hat they are wearing at the time, or the mindset through which they are approaching the sale. For example, when a woman is in her "household manager role" as she heads online, she will be researching household purchases and items for the family, including everything from birthday presents to insurance policies. At that point, being on the Internet is just another routine task and a way for her to get things done. If, however, she is online as "doctor mom," concerned with her five-year-old son's mysterious rash, for example, she will be searching for the most credible site to help her soothe her child and ease her worried mind—and she'll spend all day online, if necessary, to find her answers.

And, of course, there are the times when a woman will go online to escape stress or to self-indulge. Using the Web can become an alternate activity that helps women quickly switch gears from their day-to-day experience and take a break. So, these are the times when she is wearing her "just for me" hat and might be taking a self-discovery quiz, reading an article on a woman's site, or visiting her favorite news site.

The final role that many women regularly play on any given day is that of "Ms. Biz," when as workingwoman or business owner she is using the Web as a source for research or purchases.

Customer Experience Shapes Her Online Views

Those of us who are focused on female consumers in particular have to realize that a woman's brand loyalty truly hinges on both the product and the shopping experience. That said, our success in serving them well will depend on meeting, if not exceeding, their expectations for an improved customer relationship. Of course, just one bad online experience can ruin a customer's loyalty to the brand's off-line channel as well. All the more reason to focus in on the online customer experience!

And there can be no slacking. The early adopter and ultraforgiving online newbie days are long gone (that's so 1996). These days, most online shoppers, newbies or veterans, have higher expectations about Web-site design and customer experience. In fact, a survey of eleven thousand Internet users, including six hundred women, found that 65 percent of consumers will not shop on a poorly designed site, even if it's the site of a favorite brand.[8] Furthermore, 30 percent of the women surveyed won't use a poorly designed site, and will even cease off-line purchases from a company with a poor site, compared to 27.2 percent of men.

Shoppers who cautiously waited a while before taking their buying power online likely have that much higher expectations of how they will be served. These later adopters of the technology took their time joining the Internet masses so they could be assured that the privacy, security and service issues were already ironed out. These patient consumers were willing to wait in order to be served well when the time came, and so they are justifiably demanding customers.

Overcoming online veterans' experiences with poorly designed sites and meeting online novices' ultrahigh initial standards raises the bar for performance, design, functionality and customer experience. There's little room for mistakes in reaching the majority of online shoppers—women. Let's take a look at some of the typical online customer experience issues that women will notice:

Common Customer-Service Weaknesses

Slowness, or failure to respond, to customer inquiries.

Lack of personal contact (via an 800 number, online chat or e-mail).

Customer service staff hard to reach or find (with confusing phone tree messages or long hold times).

Customer service personnel not competent or lacking decision-making authority.

Customers required to type out complaints.

The site "Temporarily unavailable" or downloads slowly.

Top Barriers to Repeat Purchasing

Late delivery.

No order tracking, or tracking that is poorly executed.

Complicated return processes or policies.

A 2001 study of more than four thousand Web users by Brigham Young University found similar complaints to those listed in most other e-commerce studies:

General Online Shopping Complaints

Having to pay shipping charges or high shipping rates.

The difficulty of judging the quality of merchandise.

The hassle of returning unwanted items.

The possibility of credit card numbers being stolen.

Then there are the more Web-specific frustrations of online shoppers. Retail Forward, a market research firm specializing in retail and consumer product marketing, found that nearly two-thirds of online shoppers are satisfied with their shopping experiences, but more than half cited areas of frustration:

Top Five Online Shopping Frustrations[9]

Pop-up boxes when visiting or shopping a site: 52 percent

Banner advertisements: 50 percent

Congested Web pages (with ad, image or information overflow): 35 percent

Slow load times: 26 percent

Difficulty finding a specific product: 20 percent

Organize products intuitively. Forget how you organize your product line in your warehouse inventory lists. "Shop by age" and "Shop by room" are great examples of organizing products according to how people think when shopping. Make it easier for customers to find a toy that's perfect for a four-year-old, for example, and they will spend more time shopping overall.

Simplify navigation. Find objective outsiders to test drive your site and its customer experience before you go live. Since they haven't been staring at the site for several months as you have, where they get stuck on your site may be a surprise to you, revealing areas that need improving.

Trust, privacy and security. The main reasons some female consumers prefer to shop in brick-and-mortar stores include: reluctance to enter credit card data into the computer; worries that their personal information will not remain confidential and concerns about the proper delivery of their purchases. But, good online privacy and security standards have now been established, and the industry seals of approval are quite recognized (take Verisign, for example), so these concerns should be alleviated. To reach women consumers more effectively, make sure your site achieves industry standards, and make sure site visitors know that it does.

Holistic Online Experiences

Since women's brains lead them to more holistic perspectives of brands, in general, your Web site should also reflect the "whole body" of your company. The primary things women seek, of course, are high-quality products, fair prices and responsive customer service. After those are checked off their list, a woman will notice which social causes your brand supports, whether you've provided thorough background information to aid their decision-making process, whether it appears that you treat your employees and your community well and how environmentally aware your brand seems to be in its packaging.

The Saturn Corporation efffectively developed an online presence in keeping with its off-line holistic reputation. The copy from their site's "Our Story" page reads:

> Saturn was created with one simple idea: to put people first. In the beginning, our focus was on creating a different kind of company, one dedicated to finding better ways for people to work together to design, build and sell cars. A car company that talks straight does what it promises and delivers solid value at a fair price.

Furthermore, the copy on the Saturn.com site briefly describes the various partnerships it has entered into, from their strong connection with the United Auto Workers and how they work with the communities where their plants are located, to the National Education Association's Read Across America program and the National Association of Letter Carriers' Food Drive. Saturn also sponsors a cycling team, reflecting the fitness focus of their whole company.

Finally, this brand-wide attention to people, strong partnerships and sponsorships is reflected in Saturn's advertising campaigns. In a typical television spot, the brand plugs the people in their factories and local communities more than their latest models or big sale. Holistically oriented women will take all that in, whether or not they are ready to buy a car, and store that brand-knowledge for future reference.

Expand a Woman's Perspective by Serving Her Well Online

As the U.S. population ages and evolves into super-savvy Internet users, the opportunity for reaching women consumers via online channels will become huge. Whether she's a tech-aware Gen Yer, a career-focused Gen Xer or an active-in-retirement Mature woman, you should pay attention to how to reach her online, because she's bound to be there.

And, as you develop your online strategies, remember that an online woman's buying behavior can differ from her off-line modus operandi. Whether the differences are due to her comfort level with technology or her role as a household manager when she heads online, by planning accordingly you can create an effective and long-lasting connection with her.

online research

using e-marketing
to see women clearly

BECAUSE SO MANY women are already online for research and shopping, and because that number is only going to increase (remember those ultra-tech-savvy younger women), the Internet is a great place to watch, listen and learn more about women as consumers.

As we've mentioned before, if you want to learn about what matters to women, go where women are already spending time—and more and more that's online. Once there, these women may be sharing self-discovery quizzes, swapping e-mails about a particular pair of newly discovered jeans, visiting travel sites or lingering for hours on Amazon.com.

Even before you actually poll or survey women for your market research, there are a lot of ways to observe patterns, identify trends and learn the language that women use when they talk about your product or industry. Not only will those clues alone give you valuable insights, but they will also help you hone your listening skills in preparation for more traditional off- and online research.

Because a woman's view of any brand is much more holistic, taking everything in—Do I like their site? Can I find parking at their store? Is their customer service friendly? And, yes, do I like their products?—we as marketers have to take an "everything matters" approach to learning about our female customers. And, almost anything we can discover about the women we want to reach will further our listening skills.

First Sit Back and Observe Women Online

Just as the content and style of the most popular women's magazines are good beginning points for off-line research, so are the content and style of the Web sites most popular with women for online research. Whether it's DailyCandy.com for the scoop on what's hip and happening in big cities like New York and Los Angeles; a site like Tickle (at web.tickle.com) that feeds their entertainment needs; or a site that simply serves their buying needs well, like Amazon.com, there's plenty to learn about what attracts women online and keeps them there.

Using the Internet for prelistening makes it much easier to build the foundation for more detailed research. What's available online, to even a passive observer, can deliver a fairly thorough profile of your marketplace before you even start to develop your own online survey. This preparation will save you time and money to devote to the expensive, fine-tuning that will go on later in your research process.

A few passive online research tactics include:

Pattern observation. What "floats up" when you examine where women are flocking online? What do they do once there? Which tools are they using? What pages seem to be most popular? Do you notice a passionate and active feedback section? What patterns can you discern through casual observation? If there is a message board or chat area, are women using it, and, if so, what are they talking about? What seems to get them riled up, and on what days and about which topics is there a flurry of activity? What is missing from the sites women frequent? Are there fewer pop-ads or banners?

Content, color and design review. Take a look at the top ten sites your women-of-interest are visiting (include industries unrelated to yours) to see what other companies have already discovered about marketing to women.

When you identify the online focal points that seem to resonate most with women like those in your own market—whether those points involve product selection, e-commerce technology or copy style (among many other things)—you'll have gained clues to better serving your own customers. It is not hard science by any means; but this preliminary awareness-building research prepares you for getting the scoop directly from your women customers via online quizzes and surveys.

Then Ask and You Shall See (Through Their Eyes)

Thanks to the Internet, surveying and polling have gotten much simpler, and the ability to process and use the data more sophisticated. Because of the growth of the online marketing industry and the ease of online participation, people have become much more comfortable taking surveys and sharing their thoughts.

Let's start right off by admitting that online polling methods are far from perfect. Their anonymity can be great for the consumer participant, but how do we know that the respondent is really a thirty-five-year-old mother of two? And, when you are not interviewing face-to-face or on the phone, you lose important visual or vocal cues, like facial expressions and body language or pauses and clipped tones. We just have to take these limitations and variables into consideration as we evaluate the information we gather online.

In general, the Internet's anonymity means survey or quiz participants likely feel more comfortable answering personal and profiling questions. And, they'll be more likely to respond honestly too. The Internet also makes it comfortable for a consumer to participate, because she can decide when to take the time to answer the questions (which may mean at midnight).

QUIZZES AND POLLS

Online quizzes and polls are more likely to be lighter in tone and are meant to gather more wide-ranging consumer lifestyle information than more formal research surveys—prompting women to participate more for the fun experience. Women may well not even need an incentive or a prize to feel motivated to participate. Rather, it's all about whether they feel they are discovering something about themselves while they answer the questions.

Furthermore, the self-discovery quiz stimulates women's sharing and comparing that can expand the number of participants and the information you learn in a viral way. The idea is that once you learn about yourself by taking the quiz and seeing the results, you may be more inclined to share revealing information with friends and get them inspired as well.

Tickle.com offers the best examples we've seen of fun self-discovery quizzes. The capability to share and compare with friends is an attractive option that gets quiz takers returning to the site again and again. With fluff tests (like "Who's your celebrity crush?") to Ph.D.-certified quizzes (like "What's your career personality?"), Tickle.com has transformed self-discovery into an enjoyable and satisfying pastime. Even though it may be geared toward a more Gen X or Gen Y audience, there was inherent value and fun in taking the quiz even for those of us who were older. (Just finding out that our personalities matched our dogs' was all the reward we needed.)

The RealAge.com test is another online quiz that delivers value to participants, especially women focused on their health. We have found this test unbelievably compelling ourselves, and know that many other women feel the same way: The patented private, free test provides your RealAge, your body's biological age based on how well you've maintained it and your personal lifestyle. The test also indicates your age reduction benefits (what you are doing right) and makes age reduction recommendations (a personalized three month plan of what you can do to be younger, including appropriate lifestyle changes and a personalized nutrition analysis to improve your diet).

There's the benefit of increased health awareness and education from participating in the RealAge test, for certain. But, there can also be a sense of pride in finding out that your biological age may be 50, while your RealAge is only 42! (Should we pause here while you go online to take the quiz?)

The incentive for a RealAge test taker, beyond the great reports and advice at the end of the test, is that all along the course of the fairly lengthy survey you watch your age being recalculated: getting pushed up or knocked down by a few years. So, if you check the box that says you've moved in the past year, look out, you've just added a few years to your RealAge, and you learn that even before you advance to the next screen of questions. It can almost feel like a game.

On the opposite end of the spectrum of online quizzes or full surveys like RealAge's, are polls—one- or two-question quick-hit surveys that usually automatically recalculate to give you the sense that the brand is right there listening. Seeing how your answer compared to others' is fun as well. The questions in a poll may be straightforward, if not simply "yes" or "no," but they still offer entertainment value to the participant while they deliver data to the brand.

The weekly poll on StartSampling.com (see more about them below) is an example of how these polls work. The day we tried the poll the question was, what was the last thing you baked? Our answer, cookies, was the most popular response at that moment in time. Major news? No. Quirky bit of entertainment that helped us compare ourselves to others? Yes. Finally, was that poll a way for the site to collect general profiling information about its visitors? Indeed.

FEEDBACK AND PROMOTIONS

Feedback should be considered unsolicited nuggets of knowledge with twofold value: (1) You get insights directly from your customers who kindly volunteer their time to share their thoughts. (2) Your customers greatly appreciate being provided a way to submit their comments, especially if you make it clear that their input will be taken seriously. Feedback usually takes no other incentive to generate. Most people, especially women, will gladly share both the positives and the negatives, all of which are ultimately helpful for your brand's further development.

Sampling or sweepstakes offers can help begin a customer-brand connection by literally rewarding participants rather than only delivering value. StartSampling.com, for example, founded in 1998 in a suburb near Chicago, is a marketing and promotions company that has established itself as the leading online sampling company by linking brands with consumers. By offering samples of products from Nesquick Very Vanilla, Folgers and *Worth* magazine, StartSampling describes its service as "your 'voice' conduit to manufacturers," and encourages members to be candid with their opinions.

StartSampling claims it can target consumers efficiently because its shoppers and members give demographic information at registration that helps it tailor the offers they'll see on-screen. Then, a limited number of samples are offered on-screen during specific parts of the day, targeted by demographics and geography. Shoppers get samples first come, first serve, and the limited supply keeps people coming back for more: They want to be one of the first one thousand to get whatever is being given away free.

Some of the most successful tactics StartSampling has used to gather new names over time have been contests that encourage referrals. With "frequent-tryer" mile awards as prizes, StartSampling enhances the goodwill and on-site interactions. For example, someone may need to refer a few more people to get that extra number of "tryer" miles to earn the prize; so they'll keep referring. Some of the favorite gifts members have acquired through their accumulated "miles" include a Bell + Howell 35mm camera and a Home Depot 1-2-3 home improvement guide. Contests interest new members first, and then the rewards help customers realize that their feedback is indeed valued by the brands represented by StartSampling, a company that is practically a marketing-to-women best practices case study.

E-MAIL ADVISORY BOARDS

For those companies that have already compiled a database of interested consumers, there is incredible worth in continuing the conversation and maintaining that positive bond. To build an e-mail advisory board you might draw from female consumers who have participated in the course of your research, or you can invite those already actively posting feedback on your Web site. No matter how you collect these angels of insight, they can provide a wealth of information as an online advisory board.

Many customers value becoming regular "consumer advisors," perceiving and greatly appreciating the company's interest in their opinions. However, they also like feeling in-the-know, especially for the brands they love. Even though you may have paid them initially to participate in a focus group, the women who actively give you their feedback will likely continue the relationship with your brand with no further incentive. They like being heard.

Just Ask a Woman, the marketing consultancy headed by Mary Lou Quinlan, started a powerful e-mail research network they named the "Just Ask a Woman Collective," which evolved organically. Because they had met and felt valued by Quinlan in the course of her talk-show-style research and personal interviews, these same women were inspired to continue the conversation online. To express their respect for these continuing online participants, Just Ask a Woman ensures that no names will be sold and reminds participants that they can opt out of the network at any point.

While most companies do conduct research by talking directly with their customers, possibly in focus groups and sometimes on the street or on the phone, that's usually the end of the connection with any particular customer. The process of listening to your customers should be *ongoing*, not just a one-time affair. Once you've engaged a woman enough to gain her insights, she'll feel more like a part of the marketing team and naturally stay aware of your brand from then on. You'd be remiss if you let a resource like that fade into the sunset. So, build and nurture those (informal or formal) consumer advisory boards.

SURVEYS

Generally used to gather specific product or brand feedback, as opposed to overall consumer lifestyle insights, traditional surveys may be a hard draw for women consumers: Surveys are less fun than quizzes or focus groups held in a day spa, for example. By reputation a survey doesn't deliver value or fun to the participant (except for examples like the RealAge test we mentioned above). Unless there is a prior connection or reward for participating, it will be very difficult to engage women to take lengthy surveys.

That said, online survey firms like SurveyMonkey.com and Zoomerang.com have raised the bar for do-it-yourself surveys (for Fortune 500 and small businesses and nonprofits), by providing powerful software and educating marketers on how to develop questions and control survey flow, among other things. Using their services, a marketer can elicit answers to any particular question embedded in a group of less important questions, control the flow with customized skip logic or limit bias by making answer choices more random. The colors and layout of a survey can also be easily customized as well. The quick results and analysis provided by online research tools like those of SurveyMonkey and Zoomerang are great boosts toward determining your customers' true expectations and needs.

PEER REVIEWS

Sites like Epinions.com and Amazon.com provide the capability for peer reviews. Especially for women, the word of someone who is not with the company or profit-motivated can be worth its weight in gold. For example, used-car research usually involves a lot of asking around with friends who own a certain make and model, and Epinions helps expand the base of opinions that can be gathered. If you are looking for a 2000 Subaru Outback Wagon, head to the Epinions site and read experienced owner comments like: "Love the height of the outback. I don't feel like I am lying down on the floor (like a lot of wagons) and yet there's no jumping up to grab the steering wheel to get in."

In the same way, Amazon makes it easy for readers to review books and share their thoughts with potential buyers. (This can be done anonymously, so an honor system generally must prevail.) Amazon has also wisely smoothed the way for potential buyers to learn more about a particular peer reviewer, through their book reviewer ratings and the voluntary "more on me" reviewer profiles.

By encouraging or allowing for a "here's my opinion, what's yours," sites like Epinions and Amazon are building a sense of community that resonates with women. There's just something about being made to feel comfortable enough to share honest opinions.

online research dos and don'ts

DOS

▫ Pose questions in a fun, conversational tone.

▫ Package the experience as self-discovery and entertainment, where possible.

▫ Make it simple to sign in and get started.

▫ Know the incentives that will inspire responses.

▫ Express appreciation for participation.

▫ Value the participant's time. Allow opting out of surveys at any point.

▫ Keep initial surveys or interactions brief. (Gather more customer profile information later, when the participant has learned to trust you.)

▫ Use their e-mail addresses only for the originally stated purposes.

DON'TS

▫ Ask for too much personal information at the start, or ask for unnecessary personal information at all (like telephone numbers).

▫ Make your questions stiff or clinical.

▫ Spam them later once you have their e-mail address.

▫ Make surveys or quizzes too long.

▫ Abuse their generosity by requesting their feedback too often.

▫ Provide irrelevant or worthless incentives.

In order to feel compelled to continue to share her insights, a woman must feel that her participation is more than an exercise in futility. To gain a woman's trust and truly honor her time in taking your surveys or quizzes, you should frequently express your appreciation for the value of her input.

See What She Sees Online, and Learn

Observing the patterns and noticing the gathering hotspots of women online can help to quash any assumptions you may have about them and to focus your marketing approach in ways you'd never imagine.

If you knew that the women in your market were heading to RealAge.com in droves, how might that clue you in to their concerns and values? If you were an auto manufacturer and you noticed that women seemed to submit the most passionate reviews (negative and positive) of certain cars on Epinions.com, how might that help you with product development?

Just as we'd recommend that you hit the streets to watch and listen to get information about women off-line, so do we propose that you hit the sites to see what those women are discussing and what's inspiring them online. Whether it's swapping self-discovery quiz results, reviewing books on Amazon.com or participating in a purposeful survey, there are many clues to be gathered about women online that can guide your product and marketing strategy development.

Because "everything matters," especially to women, we should all remember to take that same approach as we explore the best ways of reaching them. How women behave online, including how they respond to and interact with polls, quizzes and surveys, is definitely something that should matter to us as marketers.

The clearer our marketing viewpoint, the better we can see what she sees. Online research will help keep our viewpoint, and our awareness of what interests and motivates women consumers, clean and clear.

CHAPTER 11

enlisting women as your marketing partners

an alliance for brand success

WOMEN HAVE AN incredible capacity to help solve brand challenges for the products and services they purchase. If we as marketers simply pose the right questions in the right way, we're sure to receive telling input from women like: "If you just tweaked this one product design issue, I'd be buying out the store." Or, "This marketing approach deeply offends me."

In this chapter, we will show you how to involve women sooner and more fully in product development and marketing, and we'll demonstrate why it's worth staying in touch with them on an ongoing basis. Women do provide powerful product and service insights through your monitoring of their buying behavior, but they are also very willing to help even more when directly asked. So . . . ask!

Partnering with Women to See Through Their Perspectives

For simplicity's sake, we've been referring throughout this book to the idea of marketing to women. However, as awareness increases of how women buy, there will certainly be a paradigm shift from marketing *to* women to marketing *with* women. We can no longer rest on our marketing laurels and assume or stereotype what might appeal to the women in the markets we serve. When we begin to work *with* women, it's much easier to find out what they really want and how that should be delivered.

With so many roles, life stages and life transitions affecting their buying perspective, women's needs and views are constantly evolving. So, you can't just guess what they want. Instead, invite them into your marketing research to discover their true requirements, values and preferences.

STUDY, LISTEN AND LEARN

Before you can finely tune your marketing ear to what women may be saying about your products or your industry, you should start by noting what you think you already know. Then, consider what you still need to learn. As a guide, you may want to refer to the list of twenty questions included at the end of this chapter. Your answers to those will help you communicate with female customers in a more relevant and compelling way and give you a great basis either for future listening research or for your product development and marketing efforts.

Listening, really listening, to women is the bottom line. The goal is to involve women sooner and more fully in your development of products, packaging and marketing. And, the fastest and most accurate way to learn what your women customers want is to ask them, listen carefully and see your brand through their eyes. From that vantage point you will be better equipped to make more intuitive and insightful products, marketing campaigns and advertising messages.

It may be a challenge if you've been in the corporate world for eons and using focus groups is routine. But, let's consider exploring new ways to listen to women and elevate their voices. A few listening methods to consider include:

Conversations. Don't ask women to change how they communicate; instead, change how you listen. Gathering women in informal environments like day spas and bookstores presents a more intimate, conversational-style listening option. In our own experience, we've found that such relaxed surroundings support the conversation flow and generate incredible insights on topics from making health decisions during menopause to planning lucrative retirement incomes.

Live talk-show-style listening. Mary Lou Quinlan, founder and CEO of Just Ask a Woman, a market research firm that has become known for its talk-show format, listens to women on behalf of Fortune 500 companies. The discussions are designed to respect the all-female audience and to encourage a deeper level of sharing among the twenty-five or so participants. No two-way mirrors or hidden listeners allowed, and the show is taped for future analysis. Women love to feel included and asked in this way, and the sharing and conversation is lively, fun and revealing.

Established networks. Taking a more grass roots approach than conversations and talk shows, tapping into the meetings of existing women's groups, like book clubs, walking groups, or dinner and investment clubs, can be highly effective. Established gatherings, where women have a long history of connecting to one another, often work well for discussing more personal topics. One note: Such intimate networks may not be a good choice for some financial topics, since many women may want privacy about their money issues even among friends (finding it easier to talk about those issues among strangers).

how to learn from and join the conversations of women[1]

Especially when you put them together in conversation, women have the power to help companies solve challenges, design more intuitive and relevant products, and create advertising messages that resonate—all with their usual humor and common sense. Talking with them early on produces yet another bonus, it gives them a sense that their roll in product development is active, so they will more likely be purchasers and purchase influencers as soon as the new product hits the shelves.

Tips for joining conversations with women include:

Encourage story telling. One of us (Lisa) had a college boyfriend who encouraged her to tell her stories of the day by stating her point first and then filling in the details in a logical order of importance. That way, he explained, he could choose whether to listen to the whole story. That relationship didn't last long, but mentioning the experience serves a purpose: Women share vital information about the things that brands need to know in the context of stories. So, it's not our job as marketers and researchers to ask women to sort their conversations into outlines or bullet points; rather, we must develop our ears to extract the rich information and insights embedded in their uninhibited stories. So resist the temptation to constantly interrupt and over-orchestrate the conversations (otherwise you risk validating your own personal hypotheses). If you want genuine and usable insights, you need to provide breathing room so women can get to the heart of the matter.

Use all your senses to listen. Pay attention to the energy level in the room as well as to the content of the conversation. It is important to notice when the group gets into a buzz, because then you know you've hit on an important topic or issue. When everyone starts talking on top of each other or laughing, they are having a "that's me" moment such as, "That's how I am with my kids," or "That is the state of my finances." These powerful energy shifts often provide signature stories that can form the essence of a brand's messaging.

Support the conversations through environment and context. Most research approaches don't allow women to share information in a natural way. But, fun and relevant environments can do wonders to support authentic conversations. As an example, Panasonic tested the Panasonic Pantene Ultra Ionic Hair Dryer by inviting their focus group participants to a beauty school. Each participant was given a complementary shampoo from a professional stylist-in-training, and then a new blow dryer with an assigned station and a chair and a mirror. As women took the new dryers for test-drives, Panasonic's brand managers spent time watching and interacting with participants, gathering real-time feedback and insight.

Look at her holistically. Women often view products and services as part of a solution or improvement that they will incorporate into their lives. By understanding the factors that influence a woman's buying decision along with her specific motivations for buying your product, you can gain further insight into how to position your brand.

Examine, for example, how soy milk entered the marketplace as one thing, but has since become so much more for the people who consume it. When it first hit the mainstream market, soy gave customers a lactose-free alternative to cow's milk. Then, soy milk became a popular choice with women looking to decrease menopause symptoms. And, for a whole separate reason, vanilla soy milk became popular with people who simply enjoyed the sweeter vanilla taste in their cereal and coffee. So, some milk manufacturers then caught on to this and began creating vanilla-flavored cow's milk. It just goes to show that you might think women buy your products for a certain set of reasons, but then discover that a health condition, flavor, color or even the portion size is tipping the scale in your favor. By understanding the full range of reasons people buy your product, you can form a more complete picture of which factors influence buying decisions.

Use your best listeners. When conducting research and listening to women, make sure to send those people to listen to women who understand and enjoy the market, and who are clear on the objectives of your brand. If you don't pay attention to this element of your research, the listening part of the process can end up being delegated to a professional discussion leader or stranger who may not have your brand's real interests in mind at all. Remember, it's not just what women are saying, but what the listener is hearing that will greatly affect the quality of the women's feedback you receive.

The biggest advances in joining and learning from the conversations of women will come as companies use streamlined internal communication systems (intranet and e-mail) to make the ongoing feedback from women available throughout their organizations in real time.

Virtual listening. The online world has become incredibly sophisticated in its ability to listen to women customers and learn their preferences. And, the Internet has become the perfect way to survey and connect with female consumers. The online realm provides a private way to share opinions and personal information (if the person chooses to) from the privacy and comfort of their own home.

One of the best examples of virtual listening in action is Tickle.com, a hugely successful self-discovery quiz Web destination that has attracted members tens of millions strong—roughly 70 percent of whom are women. With quizzes like "What Breed of Dog Are You?" and "Which Reality Show Is Right for You?" new members are drawn into a fun interactive experience where they involve their friends and discover more about themselves. The "word-of-mouse" factor for these quizzes is high, and members keep coming back for more, helping Tickle.com gain even more members.

While members are having a blast finding out about themselves, sponsoring companies like Unilever, Coke, Pfizer and Volkswagen are gathering important customer information (aggregated, not personalized) through the incoming data. In fact, there are billions of answers to questions stored in Tickle.com's database. Sponsor companies can begin to understand consumers through the personality profiles and aggregate information collected by Tickle.

Ask the insiders. You already know who the insiders are—the people in your industry who have important insights about your customers. So, get them on the phone and conduct interviews immediately! For even more input, you may want to assemble a panel of these experts at a trade show to discuss your specific market segment. But remember to tailor your interview requests, invitations, incentives and interview styles to meet the needs and preferences of your experts. Groups of automobile executives and gatherings of fashion journalists, for example, may find comfort in very different environments.

Internal audit. Your own customer service staff members have a wealth of information, so be sure to give their insights your full attention. Of course, some of what they mention will challenge the status quo, so make sure those you do interview have the assurance that you won't shoot the messengers. Along the same lines, you should use an outside contractor to conduct the interviews or any group conversations so that employees feel safe as the bearers of both good and bad news.

Feedback review. Via their complaint letters, e-mails and product-return records, current customers can provide valuable information to guide your brand toward communicating in a more compelling way. Remember to read the feedback from a marketing perspective (rather than the frustrated perspective of someone who has to restock the shelves, for example), and you'll gain deeper elements of truth.

Data review. You should already know where to find data on women that pertains to your industry, right? But, are you actually making a point to read it? Especially in combination with the above listening methods, reviewing that data regularly can bring your women's market profile into clearer focus.

Cross-industry research. It's amazing how connected a woman's consumer behavior may be to other elements of concern in her life. A great way to explore this is to look outside your own industry to see what women are responding to in those marketplaces. Imagine what companies in the financial services industry could learn from how a day spa or a tire company like Les Schwab operates their service businesses. There are clues to a women's buying mind and a wealth of transferable information in it all!

Women Tell It As They See It

By involving women all along the way in your product and marketing strategy development, your brand has already displayed a quality that is much appreciated by women as consumers: You respect and honor their opinions. Then, in the course of showing your respect and honor in this way, you gain all sorts of advice on what works, what doesn't, why that design is unacceptable and why this copy just resonates more.

Whether in group environments, one-on-one discussions or online, women don't need much convincing to freely offer up their inside information. Taking the time to listen and learn will help you solve brand challenges, and may even bring up a few you didn't know existed.

Often, the question for women is not simply "this one, or that one." So, let loose your research methods, drop-kick your assumptions, and allow women to share in just the ways they want to share with you. The resulting nuggets of knowledge will be golden, and your brand will shine in a similarly sunny hue.

uncovering the motivational forces of your women consumers in twenty questions[2]

This list of twenty questions will reveal the psychology of your female customer's buying mind and help you learn where your company needs to grow to more effectively reach them. But, don't pose these questions directly to your customers. Instead, do the research and answer them for yourself in order to uncover some of the forces that motivate women consumers in any market.

Answering some of them will considerably sharpen your brand. But, answering all of them will equip your brand to more powerfully connect with women in your industry.

1. What motivates women to use your product? How can you utilize these motivators to increase sales to them? How do women rationalize their purchase of your product?

2. What causes women to switch to your product and reject the competition? If they came from using a competitor's product, why did they first reject your product in favor of a competitor?

3. What are the reasons women have rejected the product in the past, and how can those reasons be managed so that they don't resurface?

4. Which of your female customers' deep, fundamental, motivating needs and desires can your company tap into? How important are their underlying desires—the ones they may not like to admit to, such as prestige, professional image, fun, luxury, wanting a change for change's sake, or fear?

5. Do women have subconscious negative reactions to your product? How can these negatives be circumvented at this same subconscious level?

6. Are messages hidden in your ads, brochures, sales presentations, demos, exhibits, events, and your customer-service style that elicit a negative reaction from women? How can they be changed?

7. If there are compelling arguments that will get women to change their minds about your product, how do they need to be presented? (By whom, through what channel?)

8. How can you disqualify the competition, reset the rules, redefine the standards, reorder priorities, change the decision-making criteria, transform the game and make your product the only one in a woman's mind?

9. What seemingly petty frustrations about products in your overall industry can you turn into major advantages for your brand?

10. What product changes are relatively inexpensive and easy for you, but offer extremely high value to the customer? What augmentations can transform a common product into a winner?

11. Are there advantages, features, benefits or company information that your marketing materials don't address, but that your female customers want to hear?

12. What are your female customers' interests and passions? Which claims, language, concepts, images and challenges inspire positive emotions?

13. What are the deeply held fundamental beliefs, values, attitudes and emotions that will lead customers and prospects to use your product?

14. What are the questions that your customers and prospects are avoiding, or afraid to ask? How can you give them the answers that will satisfy them without raising these questions?

15. What are the unexpressed expectations of your female customers, and how can they be brought more in line with what you will actually deliver?

16. What are the most effective things that your competitors are doing that you should be doing or countering? What are your competitors' vulnerabilities?

17. How can you change negative perceptions of your product without mammoth advertising campaigns? How can you capture the power of word-of-mouth referrals?

18. How is word-of-mouth, good and bad, affecting new prospects' decisions? What are the actual words used between women discussing your product and which features or benefits do they stress?

19. What are the specific steps that can be taken to increase customer satisfaction? What are the subtle things that female customers seek? Are there improvements in

service, response time or quality that would be truly meaningful to them?

20. Are your sales people really sold on your product themselves? Do your women prospects perceive a lack of enthusiasm from the sales staff?

investing in a transparent future

WE HAVE SEEN the future and I can assure you it is not pink. The path to success with this enormous market involves transparently marketing to women based on a thorough understanding of their buying behavior, insightful and innovative segmentation, and the enlisting of women as your marketing partners. A transparent approach gives marketers a new lens to look through and allows them to see lucrative and fresh new opportunities within their businesses and industries. We predict that companies who embrace and commit to transparently reaching women will position themselves for both initial success in the short term and industry leadership over the long haul. Much of the marketplace appears to be in a daze at the steep learning curve concerning what women customers want. With so much ambiguity, the prize is ripe for the picking for those companies who seize the day and engage in a transparent marketing process.

The Future of Your Business: Invest in Reaching Women

It may have been previously uncharted territory, but you can certainly proceed with confidence when considering the women's market. It will always be there and it will only grow in economic influence. Plus, even initiating an effort to understand them will be a sign that you value their business—and that's a great first step!

Beyond that, the changes you make in your products, services and customer experience will not only appeal to your most important customers (as women comprise the buying majority for most industries), but those changes will, in most cases, also exceed the expectations of your male buyers. You simply can't lose by focusing on the needs of women and tailoring your brand experience to better fit them.

Of course, getting started requires a commitment of time, talent, money and energy, but the enormous potential of the women's market has both immediate and long-term profits.

The Women's Market Investment

Invest in long-term relationships with women customers. Make a long-term commitment to improving the lives of women and serving them in a more relevant manner. Don't let your women's market efforts fizzle after the initial steps. Remember that reaching women consumers is more than implementing one big new idea. Instead, your success lies in a series of smaller and ongoing product and service improvements.

Invest in change and innovation. Many of the best ideas for reaching women have yet to be invented, and it will take employees and companies with an openness to new ideas and a commitment to internal change to bring them to the marketplace. It takes energy and commitment to turn a company (or even a team of people) in a new direction, let alone pioneer new territory with confidence and ingenuity. It is going to take a lot of change to capture the business and loyalty of the world's largest market segment, and even more change to maintain a leadership position—it is critical that organizations be willing to change.

Invest in marketing programs aimed at women customers. Until now, many companies may have talked a good game while still not committing the necessary budget in order to better reach women. In order to communicate with women in a compelling way, you need staff power, accurate information, the input of women (up-front) and key changes in the company's marketing effort—all of which take money.

Invest in capable staff. Not everyone is well suited to participating in a women's-initiative marketing team. So, pull together your most insightful, consumer-savvy, open-minded and strategic people, male and female, who genuinely like, respect and enjoy female customers.

Invest in listening and understanding. A fair number of companies are currently developing marketing plans, products and approaches around very outdated, and often untrue, stereotypes about women. Marketers need to start by listening to women and commit to involving them earlier and more deeply in the marketing process. The point-of-purchase is too late to discover the one thing any woman could have told you would kill a sale.

Invest in research. Ask yourself, "What do we think we know?" and "What do we need to learn?" Time and money should be spent to find out what is already known about your women customers, in general. Then, their personal anecdotes and details can come straight from their own mouths to amplify your research and understanding of this market.

Invest in improving and integrating the customer experience. An exceptional customer experience increases women's total satisfaction with a purchase, which encourages repeat visits and word-of-mouth recommendations. Women will be more inspired to offer you their loyalty if your company provides a consistent customer experience that meets their needs, saves them time and improves their lives.

You can feel the rumblings as companies wake up to this matchless opportunity; and we predict within the next decade key pioneers will begin to break away from the pack across all industries. In addition to scoring some immediate successes, committed companies are making wholesale changes throughout their entire organizations by embracing the transparent process. Over time we predict that these transparent front-runners in technology, healthcare, automobiles, sporting goods and consumer package goods will begin to give established Fortune 1000 companies a run for their money as they crack the code on women's preferences and buying behavior.

The transparent approach is not about isolated marketing programs, but about initiating changes that reverberate throughout an entire organization, and that point of difference gives the transparent front-runners immeasurable advantage over those who "wait and see." Women customers are opportunity number one, and with so much riding on your success in reaching them we equip you with our best advice: Don't Think Pink!

notes

CHAPTER 1

1. Hillary Chura, "Marketing Messages for Women Fall Short," *Advertising Age*, September 23, 2002, reprinted at http://www.justaskawoman.com/press.php?fn=display&newsid=23.

2. *American Men and Women* (Ithaca, N.Y.: New Strategist Publications, 2000), page 180, http://www.newstrategist.com.

3. Martha Barletta, *Marketing to Women* (Chicago: Dearborn Trade Publishing, 2003), page 7. Calculated from data from IBID Press, Camberwell, Australia, http://www.ibid.com.au. See also http://www.trendsight.com.

4. Ibid., page 5. Also calculated from IBID Press data.

5. *American Demographics* 19, no. 8 (August 1997), page 22, www.american-demographics.com.

6. *American Men and Women*, page 214.

7. "Women in Corporate Leadership: Progress and Prospects," survey report (New York: Catalyst, Inc., 1996), http://www.catalystwomen.org.

8. Federal Reserve statistics, cited in PBS Online, "To the Contrary: Women and Philanthropy—Sharing the Wealth," http://www.pbs.org/ttc/society/philanthropy.html. See also http://www.federalreserve.gov.

9. Bureau of Labor Statistics, "Detailed Personal Income," Current Population Survey, Annual Demographic Survey, March 2002. See http://www.mfea.com/InvestmentStrategies/Women/Challenges.asp.

10. Travel: "The Changing Nature of Female Business Travelers," survey by NYU's Tisch Center at the NYU School of Continuing and Professional Studies and Wyndham Hotels & Resorts, 1999, updated in 2003, http://www.scps.nyu.edu/womenbiz and http://www.womenontheirway.com. Consumer electronics: "Consumer Electronics Association Study," phone interviews with 1,002 U.S. adults in October 2003, in association with the independent market research firm Rockbridge Associates, Inc., http://www.ce.org

and www.rockresearch.com. Also see "Technology Study: Women buy more tech than men," CNN.com, January 16, 2004; http://www.cnn.com/2004/TECH/ptech/01/16/women.gadgets.ap/.

Automobiles: "American Woman Road and Travel, Auto Demographic Highlights," a female buyer study, http://www.roadandtravel.com/company/marketing/femaledemo.html.

11. "Frank About Women," *Frankly Speaking Newsletter,* vol. 1, page 1, October 2003, http://www.frankaboutwomen.com. Also see http://www.mullen.com.

12. Ibid http://www.ibid.com.au/ IBID Press, Camberwell, Australia.

13. Cited in Faith Popcorn and Lys Marigold, *EVEolution* (New York: Hyperion, 2000), page 7. Also see http://www.faithpopcorn.com.

14. Lisa Finn, editor, "Dealing with the Dark Side: Why Women's Programs Fail, and Overcoming Resistance," *Marketing to Women* newsletter (EPM Communications, Inc.), August 2003, http://www.epmcom.com.

15. Lisa Finn, editor, "Marketing Programs Aimed at Women Shows Signs of Progress, But It's Still a Sell Internally," *Marketing to Women* newsletter (EPM Communications, Inc.), December 2002, page 1, http://www. epmcom.com.

16. In 2000, the median earnings of full-time working women were $27,355, according to the U.S. Bureau of the Census; cited in *Women and Diversity WOW!* Facts 2002 (Washington, D.C.: Women's Business Network, 2003), http://www.wbni.com.

17. Mary Lou Quinlan, quoted in Randy Tucker, "Retailers Need to Listen to Women Consultant Says," *The Cincinnati Enquirer,* April 27, 2003, http://www.enquirer.com. Also see http://www.justaskawoman.com.

18. Lisa Finn, editor, "Marketing Programs Aimed at Women Shows Signs of Progress, But It's Still a Sell Internally," page 2.

CHAPTER 3

1. Anne Erickson, "Girl Power…Tools," *MSN House & Home,* reprinted 2004, http://www.houseandhome.msn.com.

2. Bob Johnson, "Women Making Home Improvements," April, 25, 2003, cited by *News Channel 9,* Chattanooga ,Tennessee, http://www.newschannel9.com.

3. Allison Wollam, "Women nailing clout with home improvement retailers," *Houston Business Journal,* July 8 , 2002, http://www.bizjournals.com.

4. Also in Alice Wollam, "Women nailing clout with home improvement retailers."

5. *The Female Home Improvement Do-It-Yourselfer Report 2003* (Tampa, Florida: Home Improvement Research Institute, 2003), http://www.hiri.org.

6. Kimberly Stevens, "Women Find Power in the Whir of a Saw," August 30, 2000, *Real Estate Journal,* http://www.realestatejournal.com/homeimprove/homeimprove/20000830-stevens.html.

7. Kimberly Stevens, "Women Find Power in the Whir of a Saw." See also http://www.builderonline.com.

8. Allison Wollam, "Women nailing clout with home improvement retailers."

9. Lis King, "Women and the Tools They Love: More women discover the joys of DIY," online article (undated), http://www.homestore.com/HomeGarden/HomeImprovement/Features/Summer/Women.asp?poe=homestore.

10. See http://www.justaskawoman.com for more about Mary Lou Quinlan and Just Ask a Woman.

11. Helen Fisher, *The First Sex* (New York: Ballantine, 1999).

12. Jackie Huba and Ben McConnell, *Creating Customer Evangelists* (Chicago: Dearborn Publishers, 2003), http://www.creatingcustomerevangelists.com.

13. Martin Lindstrom, "Online Dating—For Brands," ClickZ.com, August 5, 2003, http://www.clickz.com. Also see http://www.martinlindstrom.com.

14. Lisa Finn, editor, "Is Transparency the best policy?" *Marketing to Women* newsletter (EPM Communications, Inc.), August 2003, http://www.epmcom.com.

CHAPTER 4

1. The trends and traits outlined here are intended to offer valuable insight about large groups of women, but should by no means be considered the final word. In fact, no single behavior pattern could ever be said to fit every woman in every situation. Furthermore, the behaviors we discuss in regard to groups of women may also be true of certain groups of men.

2. See "Male-Female Brain Differences," http://www.brainplace.com/bp/malefemaledif/default.asp.

3. Turhan Canli of the State University of New York at Stony Brook, and John Desmond, Zuo Zhao, and John Gabrielli of Stanford University, "Sex Differences in the Neural Basis of Emotional Memories," *Proceedings of the National Academy of Sciences,* August 6, 2002.

4. Paco Underhill, *Why We Buy: The Science of Shopping* (New York: Touchstone, 1999), page 125 covers the related behavior of women asking sales questions more often than men do.

5. See "Male-Female Brain Differences," http://www.brainplace.com/bp/malefemaledif/default.asp.

6. Deborah Tannen, *You Just Don't Understand: Women and Men in Conversation* (New York: Morrow Publishing, 1990), page 38. Also see http://www.georgetown.edu/faculty/tannend/.

7. Christiane Northrup, M.D., *The Wisdom of Menopause* (New York: Bantam Doubleday Dell, 2001). Also see http://www.drnorthrup.com.

8. Paco Underhill, *Why We Buy: The Science of Shopping* (New York: Simon & Schuster, 1999), page 124. Also see http://www.envirosell.com.

CHAPTER 5

1. The table is based on the U.S. Bureau of the Census estimate of the total population on July 1, 2002, by age and sex (Table NA-EST2002-ASRO-01, National Population Estimates–Characteristics, Population Division, U.S. Census Bureau, Release Date: June 18, 2003, http://eire.census.gov/popest/data/national/tables/asro/NA-EST2002-ASRO-01.php). The estimates were further extrapolated based on the U.S. Census Bureau's estimate of total population on July 1, 2003 (http://factfinder.census.gov/servlet/DTTable?_ts=91919418530), which grew by about 1.0 percent over 2002—from an estimated total U.S. population of 288.0 million in 2002 to an estimated total of 290.8 million in 2003 (http://eire.census.gov/popest/data/states/tables/NST-EST2003-03.php). For simplicity, it was then assumed that each age and gender bracket grew by this same amount from 2002 to 2003; and, further, in matching up the census data with the definition of each generation, it was assumed that within each age range in the census data that the population was spread out evenly. The resulting picture summarized in the table is a good approximation of the best information available at this time.

For marketing purposes, Gen Y at the moment usually excludes those younger than tweens, that is, younger than age 6 (as of 2003). In a few years, as this generation gets older, Gen Y will probably refer to everyone born from 1980 to 1999.

According to common usage as reflected in most dictionaries, Gen X includes all those in the United States born in the 1960s or 1970s (from 1960 to 1979); but for marketing purposes, it is common to segment out those born from 1960 to 1964 as members of the tail end of the postwar Baby Boom. Thus Gen X is confined to those born from 1965 to 1979; and the Baby Boomers those born from 1945 to 1964.

Finally, then, we define all those born earlier, or before 1945 and who were age 59 or older in 2003, as the Mature generation.

2. According to *USA Today*, cited in *Women and Diversity: WOW! Facts 2002* (Washington, D.C.: Women's Business Network, 2002), page 141, http://www.wbni.com.

3. According to Teenage Research Unlimited, http://www.teenresearch.com/home.cfm. Also cited in *Women and Diversity: WOW! Facts 2002*, page 141.

4. The recent Gallup survey of youth is cited in Neil Howe and William Strauss, *Millennials Rising: The Next Great Generation* (New York: Vintage Books, 2000), page 218. Also cited in "Teens and Race," *American Demographics*, June 1999.

5. U.S. Department of Education, 2000, http://www.ed.gov.

6. Neil Howe and William Strauss, *Millennials Rising: The Next Great Generation*, page 216.

7. See http://www.quarterlifecrisis.com, and Alexandra Robbins and Abby Wilner, *Quarterlife Crisis: The Unique Challenges of Life in Your Twenties* (New York: J.P. Tarcher, 2001).

8. See http://www.emkf.org.

9. Lisa Finn, editor, *Marketing to Women* newsletter (New York: EPM Communications, Inc.), September 2000, http://www.epmcom.com.

10. U.S. Census Bureau, September 2000, http://www.census.gov/prod/2000pubs/p20-526.pdf.

11. See Lisa Finn, editor, *All About Women Consumers* (New York: EPM Communications, Inc., 2002), http://www.epmcom.com.

12. *Fall Full Year National Consumer Study* (New York: Simmons Market Research Bureau, 2000), http://www.smrb.com.

13. Jura Koncius, "Coming soon (maybe): A store for Gen Xers," *The Washington Post*, February 20, 2003.

14. See http://www.MyPrimeTime.com, San Francisco, February, 2002.

15. *Fall 2002 National Consumer Study* (New York: Simmons Market Research Bureau, Inc., 2002), http://www.smrb.com.

16. Marsha Cohen, editor, *Marketing to the 50-Plus Population* (New York: EPM Communications, Inc., 2002), http://www.epmcom.com.

17. Cheryl Richardson, *Life Makeovers* (New York: Broadway Books, 2000). Also see http://www.cherylrichardson.com.

18. See Ken Dychtwald, Ph.D., http://www.agewave.com/presentations.shtml.

19. *Tips and Facts: A Handbook to Reaching the 50+ Market*, The Business Forum on Aging, http://www.asaging.org/bfa/index.html.

20. Lisa Finn, editor, *All About Women Consumers* (New York: EPM Communications, Inc., 2001), http://www.epmcom.com.

21. Cited in Robyn Greenspan, "Senior Surfing Surges," November 20, 2003, in "The Big Picture Demographics" on http://www.internet.com. Also see http://www.nielsen-netratings.com.

22. Cited by Tam Gray, CEO and founder, Seniorwomen.com, "Who We Are," http://www.seniorwomen.com/aboutus.html.

23. Marsha Cohen, editor, *Marketing to the 50-Plus Population*, http://www.epmcom.com.

24. Ibid.

25. The Mature Traveler: 2000 Edition (Washington, D.C.: Travel Industry Association, 2000), http://www.tia.org.

CHAPTER 6

1. "The State of Our Unions 2000: the social health of marriage in America" (Rutgers Marriage Project Study, Rutgers University, 2000), http://marriage.rutgers.edu/Publications/SOOU/NMPAR2000.pdf.

2. "The Solo Female Consumer Market," *Packaged Facts* (New York: Marketresearch.com, 2001), http://www.marketresearch.com.

3. Ibid.

4. "Targeting the Single Female Consumer," *Reuters Business Insight* (London), August 1, 2000, http://www.reutersbusinessinsight.com/default.asp.

5. Ibid.

6. "Completing the Picture" (Washington, D.C.: Center for Women's Business Research, 2003), http://www.nfwbo.org/completingthepicture.htm.

7. Study in 1999 by the National Foundation for Women Business Owners (NFWBO), http://www.nfwbo.org/Research/12-1-1999/12-1-1999.htm.

8. Ibid.

9. "Reshaping the way hotels are designed and operated," female business travel survey (Atlanta: John Portman & Associates, December 2001).

10. Ibid.

11. U.S. Department of Agriculture, "Expenditures on Children by Families" (Washington, D.C.: GPO, June 2001).

12. Ibid.

13. Bureau of the Census, "Population Projections of the United States by Age, Sex, Race and Hispanic Origin: 1995 to 2050" (Washington, D.C.: GPO, 1996).

14. Study by Whirlpool, Inc., 1995.

15. Maria Bailey, CEO, BSM Media, study entitled "What's Winning the Hearts of Mothers?" http://www.bsmmedia.com/news/10ads.html.

16. Excerpt from Andrea Learned, "*Brain, Child* magazine: Where To Find A Narrow But Mighty Segment of Moms," *Reaching Women Online* newsletter, Vol. II, Issue IV, September 27, 2002, http://www.reachwomen.com/enewsletters/16.rwo.htm.

CHAPTER 7

1. For the purposes of this book, the term "Black" seemed to be the most comprehensive designation for those who are dark-skinned and of African, Caribbean or American origin.

2. Jeffrey M. Humphreys, "The multicultural economy 2003: America's minority buying power," GBEC, vol. 63, number 2, Second Quarter 2003, Selig Center for Economic Growth at the University of Georgia, http://www.selig.uga.edu.

3. M. Isabel Valdés is recognized as the founder of the in-culture marketing movement. She is also the author of *Marketing to American Latinos, a Guide to the In-Culture Approach*, Part 2 (Ithaca, N.Y.: Paramount Market Publishing, 2002). Also see http://wwiw.isabelvaldes.com.

4. Miki Turner, "The Dilemma of Aging," *Fort Worth Star Telegram*, February 9, 2003. Cited in Lisa Finn, editor, *Marketing to Women* newsletter (New York: EPM Communications, Inc.), April 2003, http://www.epmcom.com.

5. Angela Johnson, editor, *Marketing to Emerging Majorities* (New York: EPM Communications, Inc., October 2002), http://www.epmcom.com.

6. Ibid.

7. M. Isabel Valdés, *Marketing to American Latinos.*

8. Simmons Market Research, 2002, New York, http://www.smrb.com. Reported in Rebecca Gardyn and John Fetto, "Race, Ethnicity and the Way We Shop," *American Demographics*, February 2003.

9. Ibid.

10. Also see the AARP Spanish-language site, http://www.aarp.org/espanol.

11. Angela Johnson, editor, *Marketing to Emerging Majorities.*

12. Study by comScore Networks, 2003, reported in Internetretailer.com, http://www.internetretailer.com/dailyNews.asp?id=8869.

13. Angela Johnson, editor, *Marketing to Emerging Majorities.*

14. Simmons Market Research, 2002, New York, http://www.smrb.com. Reported in Rebecca Gardyn and John Fetto, "Race, Ethnicity and the Way We Shop," *American Demographics*, February 2003.

15. Study by comScore Networks, 2003, reported in Internetretailer.com, http://www.internetretailer.com/dailyNews.asp?id=8869.

16. Ibid.

17. Study in 2001 by Surveys Unlimited, a division of Horowitz Associates, Larchmont, N.Y., http://www.horowitzassociates.com.

18. Matthew Kinsman, "Invisible Giants," *PROMO* magazine (Stamford, CT), January 1, 2002, http://promomagazine.com/ar/marketing_invisible_giants/index.htm.

19. Simmons Market Research, 2002, New York, http://www.smrb.com. Reported in Rebecca Gardyn and John Fetto, "Race, Ethnicity and the Way We Shop," *American Demographics*, February 2003.

20. Ibid.

21. Ibid.

22. Deborah Kong, "Retirement Community Targets Asians," Associated Press, January 1, 2002. Cited in Angela Johnson, editor, *Marketing to the Emerging Majorities.*

23. Excerpt from Julia Huang and Lisa Skriloff, press release, Multicultural Marketing Resources, Inc., New York, N.Y., http://www.multicultural.com.

24. Ellis Close, "The Black Gender Gap," *Newsweek*, March 3, 2003.

25. Ibid.

26. Avis Thomas-Lester, "More Black Women Adopt A New Path To Families," *The Washington Post*, February 10, 2003.

27. Simmons Market Research, 2002, New York, http://www.smrb.com. Reported in Rebecca Gardyn and John Fetto, "Race, Ethnicity and the Way We Shop," *American Demographics*, February 2003.

28. Yoji Cole, "To Reach the African-American Consumer—Go To Church," *DiversityInc* (New Brunswick, NJ), December 17, 2001, http://www.diversityinc.com.

29. Kathy Bergen, "Black Papers Fight For Life," *The Chicago Tribune*, August 4, 2002.

CHAPTER 8

1. Reprinted with permission of ReachWomen, LLC, *Reaching Women* newsletter, Volume II, Issue X, 2003, http://www.reachwomen.com.

2. Sarah Ellison and Carlos Tejada, "Mr., Mrs., Meet Mr. Clean," *The Wall Street Journal*, January 30, 2003, http://online.wsj.com/home/us.

CHAPTER 9

1. According to New York-based eMarketer, Inc., as reported on Internetretailer.com, February 12, 2003, http://www.internetretailer.com/dailynews.asp?id=8626. Also see http://www.emarketer.com/.

2. Nielsen\\NetRatings, New York, May 2001, http://www.nielsen-netratings.com.

3. ComScore Media Metrix, 2002, http://www.comscore.com.

4. *North America E-Commerce: B2C & B2B*, report (New York: eMarketer, Inc., 2003), http://www.emarketer.com.

5. *Simultaneous Media Usage Study*, report (Worthington, OH: BIGresearch, October 2002, http://www.bigresearch.com. Also see the Retail Advertising and Marketing Association (RAMA), Washington, D.C., http://www.rama-nrf.org.

6. *Fall Full Year National Consumer Study* (New York: Simmons Market Research Bureau, 2002), http://www.smrb.com.

7. Paco Underhill, *Why We Buy: The Science of Shopping* (New York: Simon & Schuster, 1999), page 126. Also see http://www.envirosell.com.

8. Genex/Synovate National Customer Experience Survey, Atlanta, June 2003, http://www.genex.com/Company/News/Web_Site_Design_Affects_Consumer_Sales.html.

9. Internet Users Consumer Panel, September 2001, Retail Forward, Inc., Columbus, Ohio, http://www.retailforward.com.

CHAPTER 11

1. Lisa Johnson, "How to Learn from and Join the Conversations of Women," in *All About Women Consumers*, annual from the editors of *Marketing to Women* newsletter (New York, EPM Communications, Inc., 2003), page xiv.

2. With thanks to George Silverman, president and founder of Market Navigation, in Orangeburg, New York, for the inspiration from his original "twenty-three questions," http://www.mnav.com/default.htm.

recommended reading

Though this is nowhere near a comprehensive list of all the great information out there, the following are some of the standbys to which we turn time and again.

BOOKS

Barletta, Martha. *Marketing to Women: How to Understand, Reach, and Increase Your Share of the World's Largest Market Segment.* Chicago: Dearborn Trade Publishing, 2003.

Fisher, Helen, Ph.D. *The First Sex: The Natural Talents of Women and How They Are Changing the World.* New York: Ballantine Books, 1999.

Helgesen, Sally. *The Female Advantage: Women's Ways of Leadership.* New York: Doubleday Currency, 1990.

Popcorn, Faith, and Lys Marigold. *EVEolution.* New York: Hyperion, 2000.

Quinlan, Mary Lou. *Just Ask a Woman: Cracking the Code of What Women Want and How They Buy.* New York: John Wiley & Sons, Inc., 2003.

Tannen, Deborah, Ph.D. *You Just Don't Understand.* New York: Ballantine Books, 1990.

Underhill, Paco. *Why We Buy: The Science of Shopping.* New York: Simon & Schuster, 1999.

NEWSLETTERS/RESEARCH

Marketing to Women, monthly newsletter published by EPM Communications, New York. Covers marketing to women trends, research and intelligence that no student of the women's market could live without. EPM also publishes an annual compendium, *All About Women Consumers*, and in-depth special reports, http://www. epmcom.com.

Reaching Women, monthly newsletter from ReachWomen.com, put together by the *Don't Think Pink* authors, Lisa Johnson and Andrea Learned. The transparent marketing discussion continues in this free monthly e-newsletter, which equips marketers to better understand and more effectively reach women consumers. Subscribe at http://www.reachwomen.com and enjoy unlimited access to an extensive archive of articles.

Women and Diversity: WOW! Facts, published annually by The Business Women's Network, New York. This annual compilation of facts and figures is a one-stop resource for information relating to women and diversity in business. Available in print or online. http://www.ewowfacts.com

index

AARP, 144
Ace Hardware, 48, 49, 51, 52, 54, 62
active retirees, 106–107
Advertising Age, 3
advisory boards, online, 193–194
Aegis Gardens retirement community, 148
Ahearn, Chris, on shopping behaviors, 52
Amazon.com, 36, 188, 195, 197
Anglo Americans, 140
Asian American women, 146–150
athletics, gender discrimination in, 11–12
AT&T, 130
authenticity, 33, 41, 47–48, 53–54

Baby Boom generation, 100–105
    Internet shopping by, 175
    net worth of, 8
    senior programs for, 4
    transition market opportunities with, 167
    and visible marketing, 32
Babycenter.com, 169
Baby Einstein Company, The, 135–136
Beck, Martha, 104
Bell Mobility, 93
BIGresearch, 173
Black & Decker, 50
Black women, 150–153
Blast From the Past (film), 1–2
Bliss Spa, 42
Bolt, 92
Boost Mobile LLC, 90–93
Brain, Child magazine, 133–135

brain functioning, 63–73
    and brain synergy, 63–65
    and communication style, 71–73
    and emotional imagery processing, 58
    and observational skills, 65–66
    and sense of discovery, 67–68
    and sense of values, 68–71
Brainplace.com, 63
brand reflection
    of Asian American women, 148–150
    of Baby Boom women, 102–103
    of Black women, 152–153
    of businesswomen, 125–126
    of Generation X women, 96–97
    of Generation Y women, 87–90
    of Hispanic American women, 144–146
    of Mature women, 108–110
    of moms, 131–133
    of single women, 119
brands
    feeling of connection with, 54–55
    forming alliances with, 58–59
    fostering loyalty/trust in, 77
    improving women's lives as context of, 69–70
    life transition partnering/support by, 167–171
    loyalty to, 147
    transparent, 39–41
    understanding/definition of, 46–47, 52–53
    windows of "openness" to, 155
Builder magazine, 51
business ownership, 8, 10

businesswomen, 9, 115, 122–128
buying behavior, 73–81
  and comparison shopping, 79–81
  and constituent-driven decision
    making, 75–77
  relationships/insider information in,
    77–79
  and smart shopping skills, 73–75
  see also specific groups
buying filters
  of Asian American women, 147
  of Baby Boom women, 101–102
  of Black women, 151–152
  of businesswomen, 123–125
  of emerging majorities, 140–142
  of Generation X women, 94–96
  of Generation Y women, 85–87
  of Hispanic American women,
    143–144
  of Mature women, 107–108
  of moms, 130–131
  of single women, 118–119
buying mind, *see* decision-making
  process
buying power of women, 12

Campbell Soup, 122
CB2, 98–99
cell phones, 90–93
Chicago Tribune, 11
Christian market segment, 5
Chura, Hillary, on approach to women
  consumers, 3
churchy thinking, 5
Coca-Cola, 204
college degrees, 7
communication, 71–73, *see also* lan-
  guage(s); listening to women
comparison shopping, 79–81
competition, teamwork vs., 55–56
confidence levels, 156–158, 161–163
confident consumers, 160–161
connecting with customers
  in Baby Boom generation, 104–105
  in Generation X, 99
  in Generation Y, 92–93
  in Mature generation, 112–113
  and women as marketing partners,
    22
consumer spending, vii, ix, 9, 129, 140,
  173
contact information, 182–183

conversations, listening to, 200–203
corporate purchasing agents, women
  as, 9
Costco, 125
Craftsman Tools, 62
Crate & Barrel, 98
Creating Customer Evangelists (Jackie
  Huba and Ben McConnell), 58
cross-industry research, 205
Crow, Sheryl, 80
customer profiles, x, 12–13, 38–39
customer service, online, 179–182,
  185–186

DailyCandy.com, 188
Daimler-Chrysler, 142
decision-making process, 62–82
  and buying behavior, 73–81
  constituent-driven, 75–77
  discovery phase of, 67–68
  and gender-specific brain function,
    63–73
  and learning curves, 155–157
  during life transitions, 155–156
  motivational forces in, 206–209
  and proactive marketing, 81–82
discovery, sense of, 67–68
DiversityInc magazine, 152–153
Dodge Caravan, 69, 130
Drugstore.com, 29–30

earning power of women, 6–8
education, level of, 156–157
e-mail, 175
e-marketing, 187–197
  advisory boards in, 193–194
  and content/style of Web sites,
    188–189
  dos/don'ts of, 196–197
  feedback in, 192
  and learning from women's online
    behavior, 197
  peer reviews in, 195
  polling in, 189–192
  promotions in, 192–193
  quizzes in, 190–192
  surveys in, 189–190, 194–195
embellishments, 60
emerging majority(-ies), 139–154
  Asian Americans as, 146–150
  Black Americans as, 150–153
  buying filters of, 140–142

Hispanic Americans as, 142–146
in-culture marketing to, 153–154
emotional imagery processing, 58, 64
Enterprise Rent-A-Car, 70–71
Entertainment and Sports
        Programming Network (ESPN),
        17, 41–48
Envirosell, 177, 178
Epinions.com, 79, 195, 197
EPM Communications, 108
EQ3, 99
ESPN, *see* Entertainment and Sports
        Programming Network
ESPN: The Magazine, 43–45
evangelists, customer, 58
experience, women's buying minds
        and, 156–157, 179–182

feedback
    in e-marketing, 192
    review of, 205
    in transparent marketing process,
        39, 45–46, 51
Finn, Lisa
    on going overboard, 59
    on marketing to women, 23–24
First Sex, The (Helen Fisher), 56–57
Fisher, Helen, on web thinking, 56–57
focus, 38, 44, 49
food industry, 120–121
Ford Windstar, 41
Fort Worth Star Telegram, 141
French Meadow Bakers, 17–18, 26
Freytag, Vanessa, on marketing to
        women, 15
Frito-Lay, 122

Gap, The, 57
gender differences
    in brain function, 63–73
    in communication style, 71–72
    in emotional imagery processing, 58
    in shopping behaviors, 177–178
    in thinking, 18–19
    in tool preferences, 50–51
    and visible marketing approach,
        26–27
gender-neutral marketing approach, 16
generational characteristics, 83–113
    of Baby Boom women, 100–105
    of Generation X women, 93–99
    of Generation Y women, 84–93

of Mature women, 105–113
in visible marketing approach, 32
Generation X women, 57, 93–99
Generation Y women, 57–58, 84–93
Gillette Company, The, 16, 27, 33
Giri Choco day, 149
grade school thinking, 4–5
Greene, Sue, 162

Hallmark, 130
Hewlett-Packard, 142
Hilton, 127
Hispanic American women, 142–146
holistic approach, 184–185, 188,
        202–203
home decoration industry, 99
Home Depot, 16–18, 48, 51–54
home improvement industry, 16–17,
        48–54
Honda, 141–142
hospitality industry, 127–128
household income, 7–8
household managers, 137
household purchasing agents, 9, 75
House Rules, 99
Howe, Neil, on Gen Yers, 86–87
Huba, Jackie, on customer "evangel-
        ists," 58
human element, 168
hybrid marketing approach, 17–18, 25,
        26, 29–30

inconsistencies, 65
in-culture marketing, 140, 153–154
infant development industry, 135–136
insider information, 77–78, 204
insincerity, 59–60
Internet
    as Generation Y channel, 85
    households using, 172
    marketing information available
        from, 22
    Mature generation use of, 107
    metamarkets on, 169–170
    as tool/friend/advisor, 176
    women's view/use of, 18–19,
        173–175
    see also e-marketing; online shop-
        ping; Web sites
Israel, Richard L., on Hispanic Web
        users, 146
iVillage.com, 173

Jiffy Lube, 76
Jones Soda, 86
Journeywoman.com, 120
"June Cleaver" thinking, 5–6
Just Ask a Woman, 55, 194, 200

Kidd, Yvonne, 162
kits, 168
K-Mart, 130
Kohler, 4
Kong, Deborah, on Aegis Gardens, 148

LA Daily Candy, 77
language(s)
    of Asian American women, 146
    of brand, 40–41, 47, 57
    of emerging majorities, 140, 141
    of Hispanic women, 144
Latinas, see Hispanic American women
learning curves, 155–164
    and confident consumers, 160–161
    industry/product requirements for, 156–157
    and tentative testers, 159–160
Les Schwab, 42
life stage/role, 114–138
    of businesswomen, 122–128
    of household managers, 137
    of moms, 128–136
    and online shopping behavior, 178–179
    of single women, 116–122
    of time-challenged shoppers, 137–138
life transitions, 164–171
    brand partnering with consumers through, 167–170
    decision-making process during, 155–156
    new trends in, 166–167
    support during, 170–171
    typical, 165–166
Lindstrom, Martin, on brand alliances, 58–59
listening to women, 21–22, 199–205
Loews Vanderbilt Plaza Hotel, 127–128
Lover's Day, 150
Lowe's, 16–17, 48, 49, 51–54
Luna Bars, 122

Makita, 50
Marketing to the 50-Plus Population (EPM Communications), 108

marketing to women, vii–x, 6–24
    and changes in target market profile, 12–13
    and gender differences in thinking, 18–19
    hybrid approach to, 25, 26, 29–30
    and importance of women in U.S. economy, 10–12
    as investment in future, 211–214
    involving women in process of, see partnering with women
    as new frontier, 23–24
    new listening approaches in, 21–22
    organizational integration of, 14–15
    reframing approach for, 15–18
    and ROI measurement, 22–23
    segmentation in, 19–21, see also market segments
    transparent approach to, see transparent marketing approach
    understanding of earning power in, 6–8
    understanding of spending power in, 8–9
    visible approach to, see visible marketing approach
    see also specific topics
market segments, 4–6, 19–21, see also specific groups, e.g.: Baby Boom generation
Mary Kay Cosmetics, 70
MasterCard, 130
Mature women, 8, 32, 105–113
McConnell, Ben, on customer "evangelists," 58
McGraw, Phillip, 104
metamarkets, 169–170
Millennials Rising (Neil Howe and William Strauss), 86–87
minorities, see emerging majority(-ies)
moms, 5–6, 115, 128–136
Morgenstern, Julie, 104
motivational forces, 206–209
multisensory marketing, 56–57
music, emotional power of, 57–58

networks, learning from, 200–201
net worth of women, 8
Newsweek, 151
Nextel, 90–91

Nichols, Debra, 14
  on funding for women's initiatives, 14–15
  Web site created by, 23
Niesslein, Jennifer, 133, 134
Nike, 96
"noise," 60–61
Nordstrom, 74
Northrup, Christiane, 73
nutrition, visible marketing of, 28–29
NYC, 77

observational skills of women, 65–66
Old Navy, 87
1.5 generation, 149
online shopping, 172–186
  customer experiences shaping, 179–182
  customer services in, 185–186
  efficiencies of, 176–177
  enhancing experience of, 182–184
  expanding options for, 162
  gender differences in, 177–178
  holistic experiences in, 184–185
  information-based formats for, 68
  and Internet as tool/friend/advisor, 176
  women's roles in, 178–179
  and women's view/use of Internet, 173–175
  see also e-marketing
Orman, Suze, 39–41, 104
over-automation, 72
Oxygen, 130

Panasonic, 202
Parenting Group magazine, 168
partnering with women, 198–206
peer reviews, 195
PepsiCo, 145
peripheral brand messages, 66
personal growth industry, 103–104
personality of brand, 39–40
Peters, Tom, 12–13
Pfizer, 204
P&G, *see* Procter & Gamble
"pink thinking," vii, 1–6
polling, online, 189–192
Poshnosh.com, 111, 112
Pottery Barn, 99
pre-retirees, 106
Procter & Gamble (P&G), 14, 30

product development, involving women in, *see* partnering with women
promotions, 57, 192–193
purchasing agents, women as, 9, 75

Quicksilver, 91
Quinlan, Mary Lou, 194, 200
  on listening to women, 21
  on typecasting, 55
quizzes, online, 190–192, 204

RealAge.com, 191–192, 197
Reflect.com, 42
reframing of marketing approach, 15–18
REI.com, 177
relationship building, 155–171
  in home improvement industry, 51
  during life transitions, 164–171
  for products/services with high learning curves, 158–164
  techniques for, 78–79
  updating opportunities for, 72
  and women's confidence levels, 156–158
research, 13, 21–22, 73–74, 205, *see also* e-marketing
return on investment, measuring, 22–23
Rhodes, Jim, on home improvement industry, 49
Richardson, Cheryl, 105
Rome, Jim, 46
Ross, Patti, 23
RotoZip, 50
Roxy cell phones, 91, 92

sappiness, 60
Satellite Sisters, 104
Saturn Corporation, 42, 185
SavvyTraveler.com, 111, 112
segments, market, *see* market segments
SeniorCycling.com, 111
senior discount thinking, 4
seniors, 107
Sephora, 42
sexism, 60
Sherwin-Williams, 50
shopping behaviors, 18–19, 52, 53, 177–178, *see also* buying behavior; online shopping
single women, 11, 115–122
Sizzle and Stir, 130

spending power of women, 8–9
Starbucks, 41, 59, 66, 79–80
StartSampling.com, 192–193
State Farm Insurance, 130, 168
stereotypes, 30–31, *see also* "pink thinking"
stories, use of, 56, 72–73, 201
Strauss, William, on Gen Yers, 86–87
Subway, 60
SunnyDelight, 130
SurveyMonkey.com, 194–195
surveys, online, 189–190, 194–195
synergy, brain, 63–65

Tanabata-sama, 150
Tannen, Deborah, 71
Target, 142
target market, profile of, 12–13
teamwork, 55–56
tentative testers, 159–160
Terry Precision Cycling, 42
Theknot.com, 169
"thinking pink," *see* "pink thinking"
Tickle.com, 188, 190–191, 204
time-challenged shoppers, 137–138
time-saving aspects, promoting, 70–71
Title 9 catalog, 55
Title IX, 11–12
TiVo, 42
Trading Spaces, 99
transitions, *see* life transitions
transparent marketing approach, 25–26, 34–61, 211–212
   defining questions in, 39–41
   by ESPN, 17, 42–48
   future importance of, 35–36
   as good marketing, 36–37
   in home improvement industry, 16–17, 48–54
   keys to, 37–39, 41
   pitfalls to avoid in, 59–61
   products/services reflecting, 41–42
   secrets used in, 54–59
   as tailoring for specific markets, 34–35
travel industry, 110–113, 127–128
TravelSmith, 111
tween-years consumers, 4–5

Underhill, Paco
   on gender differences in technology use, 177–178
   on men's buying behavior, 78
Unilever, 204

Valdéz, M. Isabel, 143
Valentine's Day gift-giving, 149–150
values, sense of, 68–71
Verizon Wireless, 92
virtual listening, 203–204
visible marketing approach, 16, 25–33
visual information, 51–52
Volkswagen, 96, 204

Wachovia, 14–16, 23
wage gap, 7
Wal-Mart, 41
Walt Disney Company, 130, 136
Web sites
   consistency of retail stores and, 66
   consumer expectations of, 179–180
   content/style of, 188–189
   improving customers' access to, 174–175
   insider information features on, 77–78
   relationship-building features on, 79
   time-saving features on, 71
   see also online shopping
"web thinking," 57
Welcome Wagon, 164–165
Wendy's, 59
What Have I Done?!, 99
White Day, 149
W Hotels, 127, 128
Why We Buy (Paco Underhill), 177–178
Wilkinson, Stephanie, 133, 134
Winfrey, Oprah, 77, 103–105
W-Insight Inc., 15
Women Roar (Tom Peters), 12–13
Womensforum.com, 173
"women's initiatives," 14
workingwomen, *see* businesswomen
Wyndham Hotels & Resorts, 127, 128

Yoplait, 59

Zoomerang.com, 194–195